Dan Rice, D.V.M.

West Highland White Terriers

Everything About Purchase, Care, Nutrition, Special Activities, and Health Care

Filled with Full-color Photographs

Illustrations by Michele Earle-Bridges

BARRON'S

2 CONTENTS

WESTIE ORIGIN AND HISTORY

The elegant but bouncy West Highland White Terrier often has its rather lengthy name shortened to Westie, West Highland, or Highlander. Many terriers are named for their region of origin, such as the present-day Australian, Irish, and Manchester Terriers.

Background

The West Highland White Terrier hails from the rugged, rocky and hilly terrain in the northwestern region of Scotland, where these white dogs were selectively bred from the gene pool that also produced Cairns and Skyes. Westies' quarry hid and burrowed among rocks where little digging but great determination was needed. Therefore, the Westie evolved with a narrower, heart-shaped thorax, the better to squeeze into tiny crevices between boulders and pull varmints from their rocky lairs.

Westies were once considered a variety of Scottish terriers and were variously known as Roseneath-Poltalloch Terriers, White Cairn Terriers, or White Scottish Terriers. In an 1887 publication, the author of which is unknown, Westies reportedly weighed 16 to 20 pounds (7.25–9 kg)—(the same as today), and were ". . . determined vermin-destroying dogs . . . well knit together, between cobby and long,

"Is this book about me?"

but very deep . . . They stood on short bony legs, the front ones being quite straight . . . were linty white in color and with a hard and bristly coat." The report continues, "I know exactly what those dogs are fit for and may add that no water was ever too cold and no earth ever too deep for them."

The famous Crufts dog show in 1907 was the setting for the Westie to make its first appearance as a show dog. Westies came to America when Robert Goelet imported Ch. Kiltie and Rumpus Glenmohr. From the very first Westie to step on United States soil, these lovable little dogs established their reputation as excellent companions with a built-in propensity to rid their surroundings of vermin. The West Highland White Terrier Club of America was admitted to AKC membership under the name of Roseneath Terrier Club in 1908, and the next year it was changed to its present name. Since about 1960, Westies have regularly gained popularity and today rank in the top third of all AKC registered breeds, second only to the Miniature Schnauzer among the terrier breeds.

Character and Disposition

Hardy West Highlanders have enjoyed great popularity as rugged outdoor companions, and their amusing, lighthearted, and mischievous ways have won American hearts by the drove.

Westies are quite sociable, the merriest and most cheerful of Scotland's terriers, having a pronounced optimistic outlook on life. They have the endurance of a much larger dog and owners need not pamper them or carry them home from a long walk. Often described as intrepid, this diligent and alert little dog is loyal and extroverted, truly a giant in a compact package. An independent thinker usually has its stubborn streaks, and the intelligent Westie is cunningly autonomous. Extremely self-confident and assured, the Westie isn't easily impressed by unimportant matters.

Built into every alert Westie is an alarm that can be triggered at any time by any disturbance; thus they are excellent watchdogs. Most Westies are wild about balls or other small toys and if encouraged, will play by the hour. The Highlander is an enthusiastic and ambitious pet with instinctive earth-dog characteristics. Its curiosity and ambition are driven by the need to investigate and approve of everything in its environment, and this need is satisfied daily with enthusiasm and vitality.

Bold and energetic, the Westie is self-assured, yet exceptionally loyal. He was bred with human interests close to his heart and he wants to be with his family every minute. His amusing antics will win out and make correction extremely difficult. A Westie has a optimistic nature and endless energy that may cause conflict with some owners. Truly, the Westie is not the dog for everyone. A typical Highlander demands ceaseless commitment to lessons, exercise, and games. He will benefit from regular obedience tune-up sessions that will enhance your appreciation of your relationship considerably.

The Westie's perpetual animation will frustrate, yet entertain, delight, yet vex. If this type of relationship doesn't appeal to you, please consider another breed. Before you buy, learn as much as possible about terriers in general and Westies in particular. Never imagine you can mold this canine personality to suit yourself; some inherited traits are stronger than human will.

Terrier instincts are always present in Westies.

*Westies and cats should
be introduced carefully.*

Neglect, boredom,
and lack of human
attention will
ruin a nice
Westie and stim-
ulate objectionable
vices. Some humans
enjoy teasing small dogs
just to cause them to bark or
dig and bite at the restraining fence. Teasing is more damaging to a terrier's personality
than neglecting it.

Sociability

Somewhat pugnacious around strange dogs
and small animals, the Highlander is generally
sociable with friendly dogs and family cats, but
this little dog with the big attitude isn't likely
to be intimidated by the barking of the neighbor's Great Dane. He'll escape from your backyard to follow a badger to ground if one can
be found, and if not, he will probably settle for
the neighbor's ferret, a stalwart chipmunk, or
your pet gerbil.

The occasional strong, masculine (alpha male) personality
of some male Westies tends to
erupt when another male is
introduced. Usually this charac-
teristic is amenable to change
by castration of pet Westies.
Fights are rare between

*A Westie will not back
down from any dog.*

neutered males or females that have been
raised together or that are carefully introduced. These conflicts often are associated with
jealousy and can be controlled by equalizing
your handling and attention.

Breed Standard

The official West Highland White Terrier
breed standard is quite complex. If you're considering purchasing a breeding or show-quality
Westie, you should write to the

Just a lovable li'l Westie.

"Let's go have some fun."

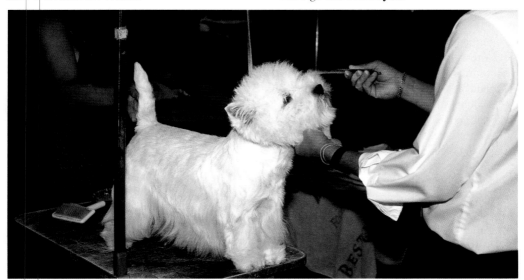

"What we won't go through to win."

Now this is the way Westies are supposed to look.

Westies are always ready to play.

As Scottish as it gets!

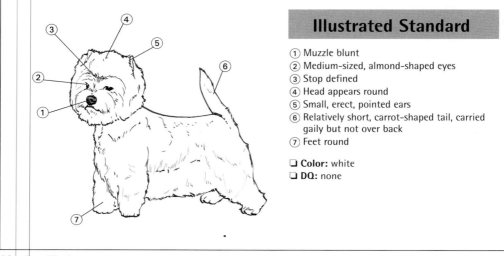

Illustrated Standard

① Muzzle blunt
② Medium-sized, almond-shaped eyes
③ Stop defined
④ Head appears round
⑤ Small, erect, pointed ears
⑥ Relatively short, carrot-shaped tail, carried gaily but not over back
⑦ Feet round

❏ **Color:** white
❏ **DQ:** none

DQ = disqualification

American Kennel Club (AKC) or the West Highland White Terrier Club of America (see Information, page 92), or obtain the official standard from the Internet. Westie faults are fully covered in the official standard, as are the specific virtues both of conformation and temperament. Those who want only the basic information extracted loosely from the breed standard to help them choose a pet-quality puppy will appreciate the following description.

General Appearance

The Westie is a game, hardy appearing, compact terrier with loads of self-esteem. Standing 10 or 11 inches (25–28 cm) tall on sturdy legs, its anatomy is muscular, its chest is deep, its back straight, and its hindquarters powerful. The Westie's athletic body is covered with a hard, white coat about 2 inches

(5.1 cm) long with an abundant softer under-coat. The body hair is usually plucked and trimmed for shows, but left longer on the head, which adds significantly to the Westie expression.

The Westie's roundish head and inquisitive expression are enhanced by wide-set, dark brown, almond-shaped eyes rimmed in black. The Westie's skin also is darkly pigmented, and his ears are small and naturally pointed.

The teeth of the Westie are larger than those of similar-sized dogs, and the dentition must contain six incisor teeth between each pair of sturdy canines. A scissors bite, with upper incisors slightly overlapping the lowers is required.

The Westie's muscular neck and flat, level topline are significant, and the Westie's com-pact body is of good substance. His chest is very deep and his loin is short and strong, finished with a relatively short, carrot-shaped tail that is carried straight up and never curving over the back.

Correct angulation of both front and rear is important, and his well-boned forelegs are relatively short and muscular. Rounded forefeet are larger than the hind ones, and all four are equipped with thick black pads and strong claws. His relatively short, muscular hind legs are parallel, having well-angulated hocks. The free and easy gait of this athletic terrier is reaching, powerful, and smooth, with his back remaining level when moving.

Coat

A great deal of emphasis is placed upon his double-layered coat, the top of which is hard and wiry, in contrast to his soft, short undercoat. Westie skin tends to be drier than that of most dogs, which is why they have very little doggy odor. Plucking instead of clipping is necessary to achieve excellence in blending the softer undercoat with the longer, harder topcoat. A soft, fluffy, flyaway coat is undesirable

TIP

Westie Appearance

The Highlander is a clean and tidy housedog. Its snowy white coat, curiously mischievous expression, liveliness, small, pointy ears and jet-black facial accouterments set it distinctly apart from other terrier breeds.

and will be the difference between a winner and loser in the show ring. Sometimes blamed on faulty grooming, a silky coat, or one tending to curl, may mark the end of a Westie's show career before it starts.

Temperament

Temperament is critically important, and an excessively timid or pugnacious Westie only receives judges' cursory glances. Typically alert, courageous, with a large measure of self-esteem, the Westie is outgoing and friendly.

FINDING THE BEST WESTIE

Don't even think of buying your Westie until the breed and breeder have been thoroughly investigated and all your questions have been answered. If you're planning to buy Duff for your small children, don't! Baby Westies and baby humans are not always a good combination.

Timing

If your kids are older, and you want a surprise to put under the tree on Christmas morning, buy an electric train.

✔ Don't invest in a puppy until every aspect of dog ownership has been discussed with the entire family and agreement is reached about Duff's training, feeding, exercise, and health care. Never buy a dog as a surprise gift, especially if you only *assume* the recipient will love Duff. Perhaps the person had another breed in mind; maybe a Westie is too small or the wrong color.

✔ Don't bring Duff home when his care must compete with the excitement of holiday festivities, nor when an ensuing vacation will take the family out of town for a couple of weeks. Have you ever tried to housebreak a puppy on a drive to Disneyland?

✔ Don't count on boarding Duff because reputable kennels have rules prohibiting keeping young puppies before they've received all vaccinations. Duff won't be boarded until a

"Just whose bowl is this?"

veterinarian certifies his health and even then his exposure to strange dogs is ill advised.

✔ Obtain Duff at a time when you have a week or at least a few days to spend with him. Taking a week's vacation from work may seem like overkill but don't forget this is a long-term investment, and one you should protect.

✔ Don't delegate the first few days in your home to anyone who isn't dedicated to Duff's well-being, his housebreaking, and his first real social contact with humans. The first days are critical and if handled incorrectly, the scene can be set for years of troubled ownership.

Are You Ready for a Westie?

When you consider buying a puppy, think carefully about what you're doing before you commit. Are you willing to take *total* responsibility for Duff's care? Children's priorities often change, and what they're dying to undertake today, they disdain tomorrow. Your spouse may change jobs next week and be unable to share Duff's care. Remember the family's dynamics;

children grow up, you move to an apartment in another city, a promotion means more money but less free time, or you break a leg and have plenty of time, but poor mobility. Your new Westie still will require several hours every day for training, grooming, exercise, and feeding.

Many modern families must schedule and prioritize their time and sometimes none remains for a pet. Don't act on speculation that you'll have more time next year. Delay Duff's purchase until adequate time can be afforded him.

As a workable option, consider a time-share plan. A child takes charge of Duff's feeding, and another is responsible for a half-mile walk in the morning. Your spouse agrees to walk him in the afternoon, and a child cleans up the yard. You take him for vaccinations, to training classes, and tune him up when necessary, and your parents will keep him when vacation time rolls around. This may relieve you of total responsibility but is an option that might work in your family. Here are some important questions.

✔ Have you a safely fenced space for a dog's play and exercise?
✔ Do you and your spouse have sufficient income to afford a dog?
✔ Will you commit your time to Duff's daily socialization requirements?
✔ Will you acquire the knowledge to teach him good manners and basic obedience?
✔ Will your humor and patience give way to a short temper?
✔ When you travel, will your Westie be given plenty of human companionship?

Good Westie Breeders

By arbitrary definition, a reputable Westie breeder is associated with a local all-breed club, or regional Westie club and possibly a member of the WHWTCA. A reputable breeder is certainly one who raises only the number of litters that can be properly handled. Usually that amounts to no more than a couple per year because each Westie puppy must receive abundant human attention from whelping time until it's sold and must be socialized apart from the other puppies. A reputable breeder is one who stands behind each puppy with a guarantee of good health, effective socialization, and freedom from congenital defects.

A pedigree and a document that fully explains return privileges should accompany each Westie puppy sold. A reputable breeder will have a contract for buyer's and seller's signatures that defines both parties' responsibilities. An accompanying sheaf of papers will describe everything you need to know.

Westies, like all terriers, love to dig.

The Web

Finding a reputable Westie breeder is a challenge, especially in this computer age. Many breeders have web pages complete with pictures. Let's face it, in two dimensions, most Westies look alike and personalities aren't visible in photographs. All breeders aren't equally honest; don't ruin the next dozen years of your life by purchasing your companion from an Internet picture or claims made by an unknown and perhaps unproven breeder. However, breeder ads found in magazines or on the Internet might be an excellent *starting* place. In addition to searching the Web for breeders, go to the AKC page or to the WHWTCA page to locate the secretary who can assist in your search and give you the names of reputable breeders in your locality. If you contact a breeder by phone, ask to see available puppies but don't buy from the first breeder you visit.

Dog Shows and Trials

Whether you're looking for a show dog or a pet, you should first attend a dog show, an obedience trial, agility contest, or earthdog test to meet and talk with Westie breeders and fanciers. After you've studied many excellent Highlanders and are satisfied that it's the right breed for you, pick several breeders with good reputations and winning dogs, and visit them. You should consider a breeder's success in whichever aspect of Westie ownership appeals to you as well as the appearance and personality of pups offered for sale. Whether your chosen companion is perfect or slightly less, don't settle for one with obvious congenital deformities or a questionable personality.

Ask the breeder if boarding is possible in case you aren't able to take Duff with you on vacation. It would be wonderful if his breeder would care for him in that event. Expect to pay for this service and ask what the boarding fee will be.

Newspaper Ads

Amateur or backyard breeders often dominate classified ads. Telephone before you visit these litters, ask the ages of the parents, and quietly reject pups whose parents are less than two years old. Backyard breeders often own both parents. Ask if the sire or dam has participated in any type of competition. If they haven't, be

━━ CHECKLIST ━━

Questions Often Asked by Breeders

1 How much spare time do you have?
2 Do you intend to show or enter dog sports?
3 How big is your yard, and is it fenced Westie-tight?
4 Do you have any other dogs; if so, what breed, what sex, and how old are they?
5 Do you have any small pets such as cats, birds, ferrets, or gerbils?
6 Have you ever owned a terrier before?
7 Have you ever trained a terrier?
8 Do you intend to breed your dog or have it neutered?

If your responses to these questions aren't acceptable to the breeder, you might find yourself at the bottom of the list of prospects for a new Westie.

very skeptical, because backyard parents rarely are exhibited in any serious competition. Ask if the puppies' parents have any bad habits; if the breeder tells you they have none, skip quickly to the next ad. Ask if the dam and sire are closely related and if both are AKC registered and pedigrees are available to see.

Perhaps you aren't considering AKC competition when looking for a pet, but your attitude may change as Duff matures into a beautiful, intelligent, and trainable adult. A backyard breeder's puppy may have an acceptable temperament, conform reasonably well to your idea of the breed's general appearance, and have other qualities of a pet-quality Westie, but a significant risk accompanies purchase from a backyard breeder. The puppy may have inapparent hereditary diseases or apparently minor faults that will blossom into large problems in the future.

"I'm just helping celebrate the season."

A Family Dog

All Westie owners want a good-looking pet. They're seeking a superintelligent puppy, a beautiful representative of the breed, one that has a fabulous personality and is easily trained, but not necessarily a dog with exhibition potential. An extremely high percentage of all buyers want the best Westie available—within their price range. They're true fanciers and love the terrier personality, but only a small number are interested in showing their Westies.

Most of these amazing little white dogs are happily getting underfoot and playing with the kids and are quite at home on laps of every dimension. Westies provide needed exercise for couch potatoes who prefer watching soaps instead of waistlines. Westies are loving and well-loved companions that entertain children, play Frisbee with teenagers, jog with yuppies, and share senior citizens' golden years. They stimulate aging interests by demanding attention and initiating visits to neighbors, nursing facilities, and care homes.

A Great Companion

Inexperienced shoppers select their companion with less consideration than they give to their choice of a roast for Sunday dinner and simply toss the first one seen in their grocery basket. Picking the best Westie is an art! Seek yours from good parents that have been raised by loving people. Choose from dogs of high quality that have been proven in shows or other Westie activities, because these dogs are among the best representatives of the breed.

Choose your puppy from a dam with a great personality, one that has all the attributes you want in your companion. Look for friendly, outgoing puppies that are playful and curious. Don't select your Westie from the first litter you see; you'll be surprised at the differences between puppies from several kennels.

Westie Cost

Usually, purebred Westies are sold on a scale that includes show and breeding prospects at the top of the cost curve. Purchase price may depend on you and your family's age and experience, the type of home you'll give the puppy, the facilities and training you promise to provide, and your expectations for her. If you're interested in showing or exhibiting her,

share this fact with the breeder before you visit. It's possible the breeder will consider co-ownership of an outstanding puppy, providing you're able and willing to train and exhibit her.

Ongoing Costs

Tammy's initial cost is only the beginning. Ongoing costs often are greater than expected. Check with a veterinarian about fees for vaccinations, spaying or castrating, annual booster vaccinations, parasite control, and other preventive health care. Investigate the cost of insurance to insulate against emergency needs. Ask about training expense, cost of puppy kindergarten, and boarding fees if you can't take Tammy with you on vacations. If you're planning for a hired dog walker or dog sitter, investigate the cost of those services as well.

Good breeders are dedicated to raising healthy puppies.

Age to Acquire Your Westie

Most reputable breeders' puppies are available from two to four months of age. By this age, Tammy will be well socialized with siblings and parents in her nest environment, and human socialization is begun as well. Ideally, you should obtain Tammy soon after she is weaned and eating solid food. She'll have experienced an abundance of human handling, cuddling, and petting, and the bonding wheels are turning. Bonding is possible at any age, but the period from three weeks to three months is the most important.

If you find a viable puppy and she's four or five months old, don't worry; just be sure she's been handled by adults and children and is well socialized with humans. Don't accept a puppy that has been kennel raised for several months in exclusively canine company.

Even at an early age, Tammy will be as anxious to wrestle with the kids as they are to play with her, but take care that your young Westie is handled gently. Both fragile bones and temperament are at risk. Her character is forged by early handling, and repeated errors made by children can be quite difficult to remedy.

TIP

Neutering

When considering neutering your pet, remember that spayed females and castrated males aren't eligible for certain AKC events. Be sure to address this with the breeder at the time of purchase.

Children's time spent with Tammy should be carefully monitored, and children under the age of six or seven must be taught that Tammy should be left on the floor and picked up only by adults.

Adopting an Adult

An adult Westie may appeal to you. Mature terriers sometimes are available from pounds, shelters, and rescue agencies. Occasionally, an adult may be obtained from a breeder who has an older show dog in good health, one that's ready to retire to a good home. Investigate this possibility, and while you're at it, ask breeders and veterinarians about problems you might encounter with Westies from rescue groups or shelters. However, if you're inexperienced with rescue dogs and are short of time or patience, leave those dogs to experts.

Never adopt a mature Westie from any source without return privileges. Leave a deposit, obtain a contract, and try Tammy in your home for at least a month. Prior abuse or neglect will make successful rehoming more dubious. From the very first it is extremely important to establish consistency and trust. To succeed with a rescue dog, treat her with respect and love, give her as much of your time as possible, and be patient. Reward her when she's right and ignore her when she's wrong. This Westie is carrying baggage from her past and must adjust to an entirely new environment with new people, different restrictions, and dissimilar lifestyles.

An adopted adult may be on her best behavior at first and her vices won't surface for several weeks. Her training and learned habits are already molded into her personality and will be remembered. Unacceptable behavioral traits respond slowly to adjustment but with the exception of instinctive traits, habits can be altered. Give her ample opportunity to adapt to your home but don't expect miracles. Adopt her at the end of her probationary period only if she's showing signs of compromise and is beginning to adjust to your lifestyle.

However, if she's resisted all your affection and every attempt to establish her trust and her bad habits persist, give it up. Some Westies refuse to cooperate and it's unfair to you and your family to waste more time with a dog that will never make a satisfactory pet.

Male or Female?

Either sex will be a good companion if it's neutered, trained with love, and lavished with as much attention as you can give. Personality differences and appearance are inconspicuous between males and females. Some breeders suggest that males make the best pets in spite of their instinctive masculine traits. Aggressiveness will be changed when neutered. Initial cost differences between males and females usually are insignificant when choosing a pet-quality puppy.

Spaying

Spaying Tammy isn't just an arbitrary birth control program. The surgical procedure removes both ovaries and the uterus (ovariohysterectomy) to extend her life by preventing several serious diseases. The operation is done under general anesthesia with few complications. Minimal hospitalization time is required and within a few days she should act and eat normally.

CHECKLIST

Puppy Papers

Be aware of the following papers you should receive with your pup.

1 AKC puppy registration document, ready for you to submit to AKC.

2 AKC pedigree.

3 Vaccination document indicating vaccination date, by whom given, and when booster is due.

4 Results of most recent worm check and if wormed, what product was used.

5 Dietary information, including when, how much, and name of food being fed.

6 In many cases, a contract is signed that might include your agreement to have Tammy spayed by a particular age.

7 A written guarantee of her health should state the duration of the guarantee and your options should be specified if she is not found to be in good health. If on veterinary examination she is found to have a previously unidentified defect, the contract should state that you have the option to receive your money back or a replacement puppy (within a specified time) from this or another litter. If Tammy or her siblings have been ill, call the doctor and discuss the illness before you agree to purchase her. Ask if her illness has any future significance, and whether she should be examined to confirm her total recovery.

Spay Benefits

✔ She no longer has three-week heat cycles twice a year.
✔ She doesn't become pregnant.
✔ If spayed before her first heat, breast cancer rarely occurs.
✔ Spaying precludes development of hormone-related diseases such as pyometra and endometritis.
✔ Spaying doesn't change Tammy's personality, ambition, trainability, growth, or development rate.

Castrating

Castration Benefits

Castrating a Westie entails the surgical removal of both testicles. Recovery should be

"A clean environment is okay, but these flowers are too much."

uneventful and rapid, and within a day or two he'll be playful and hungry.
✔ Aggressiveness toward other males is reduced.
✔ Testicular tumors, prostatitis, and prostatic cancer are averted.
✔ Castration curbs the desire to escape from your yard to search for females in heat.

Age to Spay or Castrate

Many veterinarians recommend spaying females at five to six months of age. If done before the first heat, the threat of breast cancer is virtually eliminated. Pet Westie males usually are castrated at about 8 to 12 months. However, it's quite feasible to spay or castrate

"Nobody move till we get the cat out."

a much younger dog and the techniques are reported safe, effective, and without personality problems. Recently, puppies in shelters have been sterilized as early as 12 weeks of age without complications, and in 1993 the American Veterinary Medical Association formally approved early neutering of puppies and is apparently satisfied that it doesn't affect growth rate, food intake, or weight gain. This has led to changes in the opinions of some breeders and ethologists (behavior scientists).

It's probably too soon to unequivocally support early sterilization, but present experience and research indicates no significant negative impact on either physical development or personality, and the practice has greatly reduced euthanasia in American shelters and pounds.

A Happy, Healthy Puppy

Never purchase a puppy because you feel sorry for her. She might not be a perfect Westie according to the breed standard but her health should be unquestionable. Tammy will be with you for many years and if she isn't robust when purchased, she may never be sound. With the seller's permission, leave a significant deposit and take Tammy directly to your veterinarian for a prepurchase exam.

Be aware of the Westie breed's propensity for skin disease when you're evaluating a litter. Skin problems are sometimes inherited, and if you see puppies with patchy reddened skin, hasten out the door! If a litter is kept in a dirty environment or poor sanitary conditions, leave before you're tempted. You're entitled to choose from a healthy, well-nourished, playful litter of puppies that are housed in a clean environment.

HOW-TO: RECOGNIZE A

Personality and temperament should be evaluated in addition to physical health. On your first visit, sit on the floor and let the puppies climb on your lap and wash your face, and note any that hide shyly. Toss a paper wad and watch the puppies chase it, making note of any that aren't interested. Roll a soda can with a few marbles inside and note any frightened puppies. Watch for subtle individual differences in temperament. One puppy may be consistently more aggressive, another might display more mischievousness or curiosity, and another may be overly active. When you've reached the final selection stage, watch the litter secretly. Stand out of sight behind a door and peek through the crack. Choose a puppy that's laid back, yet curious, mischievous, yet not overly aggressive, bouncy but not hyperactive.

Pick up your selection and walk into another room, sit on the floor, and place her beside you. If she immediately climbs on your lap and covers you with wet puppy kisses, wagging her tail energetically, you've probably found a good match. Then hold her upside down in your arms and rub her tummy. If she accepts that without excessive struggling, she's yours!

Here are the physical signs of a healthy Westie:

✔ Her dark eyes should be clear, without redness, tearstains, or pus.

✔ Her gums, tongue, and palate should be moist and bright pink.

✔ Her teeth should be white, never stained with brown patches. The upper incisors should close over and touch the lowers.

✔ Her ribs shouldn't be visible but should be easily felt under a thin layer of fat.

✔ Her abdomen should be full after eating, but she shouldn't have a potbelly.

✔ Her skin should be supple, neither leathery nor dry, and no hairless areas or redness of skin should be seen. Repeated scratching may be cause for alarm.

✔ The hair around her anus should not be stained with feces, which might indicate diarrhea.

✔ The joints of her legs should not be overly enlarged or tender to mild pressure, and her forelegs should be straight. (If you are unable to decide about joint size, ask your veterinarian's advice.)

✔ Her pasterns (the joint just above the toes) should be

A healthy Westie is brimming with vitality.

vertical and strong, never soft and yielding resulting in a slump in her gait (down pasterns).

✔ When standing still, her toes should be gathered together, not splayed, and her feet and hocks should point straight forward and backward, not inward or outward.

✔ Her movement should be a normal, straight, smooth gait, without any sign of lameness.

✔ Be suspicious of any pup that remains quiet when her siblings are playing.

✔ Don't choose a puppy that dominates its littermates at the food bowl, is unusually quarrelsome or growls as it stands over its siblings.

Healthy puppies will be easy to spot when you're looking at a litter.

Congenital Defects

If you notice a marble-sized enlargement in the center of her abdomen, it may be an umbilical hernia that could require surgical repair in the future. This minor problem shouldn't affect your choice, but the breeder might lower the price to compensate for the surgical fee. If the puppy is a male, his testicles should be descended into the scrotum by weaning age. If you can't find them in place, mention it to the breeder and discuss it with your veterinarian when the puppy is examined. If buying a show prospect, be absolutely sure both testicles are in the scrotum, and if in doubt, wait a week or have him examined by your veterinarian. If he's being purchased at a pet-quality price, the hidden testicles can be surgically removed.

Circulatory defects are invisible without the help of a veterinarian's stethoscope, but a puppy is suspect if it is smaller than its siblings and lacks the stamina of the other puppies.

Some litters include a puppy that is notably smaller than the others and is commonly referred to as a *runt*. If you are looking for a pet and a veterinarian has examined this puppy and declared it sound and healthy, it might be considered. Similarly, if one puppy is larger than all the rest, but appears normal in other respects and has been examined and passed by your veterinarian, it should be considered.

PREPARE FOR YOUR WESTIE

You'll undoubtedly make your home a pleasant one for your new pet, but by all means, be sure to make it as safe as possible for her.

One Room at a Time

Puppy-proofing your entire home may be impossible, so tackle the job one room at a time. If a 10-week-old Westie suddenly enters your home, what can she get into? A better question might be, what hazards to her health might be eliminated before she arrives? If you've decided she's to be primarily kept in the kitchen because it's a large room that's easily cleaned, remember the odors that accompany little Westie accidents left on the floor. Sanitation is sometimes a challenge, and there's always the problem of having Tammy under your feet when you're trying to prepare meals. In many modern homes, the kitchen is merely an extension of another room, with no clearly defined doorway, so perhaps your kitchen isn't a good room to choose.

A bathroom? An easily cleanable bathroom or laundry room often suffices for a nighttime housebreaking enclosure if you don't have a pen or crate, but isn't it a bit remote from the family? How often can you bend down and pet her, or pick her up for a quick cuddle?

Before Tammy makes her initial appearance, decide where her sleeping crate is to be placed so she always has access.

A logical answer to this dilemma is to close the bedroom doors, block the stairway with an infant-proof gate, and put another gate at the entrance to the dining room and rooms with breakable or chewable items, if possible. Then allow Tammy to follow you around, chew your shoelaces, and get underfoot. You'll be able to talk to her, sympathize and cuddle when she's pushed from your path. She'll learn where to sit safely, and you'll keep a vigilant eye on her for signs of impending urination or defecation. Soon you'll learn to shuffle your feet and watch where you step, and the two of you will become intimate buddies.

Chewing

Tammy's propensity to chew dictates that you remove temptations.

Every Westie is a natural-born explorer.

Stairs should be off-limits to puppies.

metal "squeaker" can be plucked out, swallowed, and surgery may follow. Nontoxic crayons have an extraordinary appeal to the tiny puppy; they're soft and small enough to chew up and swallow, and much to your astonishment, they lend a kaleidoscopic appearance to her next few bowel movements.

Backyards

Tammy needs a big yard to give her plenty of room to burn off her energy. Tammy's requirements can also be met with several long walks a day and perhaps a trip to the park every day or two. Vigorous playtimes and training sessions in the living room or on the roof may contribute to burning up her energy. Apartment dwellers have proven their ability to live harmoniously with an energetic Westie.

Fences

Your backyard should be fenced Westie-tight and be maintained in good repair. These little guys are talented escape artists and can wriggle through the smallest of holes or find a soft spot to squeeze under. In some regions of the country, block fences are popular. Although they certainly confine dogs quite well, Tammy may run up and down, becoming frustrated by her inability to see out. If that's the design, try having a few decorative blocks inserted to afford her a look at the outside world. Board

✔ Appliance cords must be disconnected or fastened out of reach.

✔ Remove live and artificial plants from her reach.

✔ Sweep up all crumbs from under chairs, lest she develop an insatiable appetite for animal crackers and apple sauce.

✔ Relocate your first editions from the bottom shelf.

✔ Be sure table scarves are tucked up well above her reach.

Kids' Toys

Kids' toys are an ever-present attraction to Tammy, and some may be quite dangerous. Small soft rubber balls are capable of causing intestinal blockage if the ball or pieces of it are swallowed. Squeaky toys should never be allowed within your Westie's range. Tammy's sharp teeth can easily rip the hollow rubber; the fences obscure her vision except that often they're sprinkled with knotholes to peek through. Unfortunately, they're chewable and sometimes coated with toxic preservatives. Chain-link fencing is an excellent choice, but it may allow your tough little friend to challenge neighborhood dogs and encourage barking at mailmen, visitors, and meter readers.

Digging

All terriers dig. Indeed, most dogs of any breed find satisfaction in burrowng in soft earth. An inexpensive addition to your yard that will be most appreciated is a digging ground. Pick a spot about 6 feet (2 m) square at least a yard (1 m) from the fence, and far away from your vegetable or flower garden. Haul in a few wheelbarrow loads of clean sand (from a builder's supply house) and spade the sand into the already present topsoil. Hide a dog biscuit just beneath the soil's surface while Tammy is watching you. Then watch the sand fly! You can use this digging ground in various games, hiding her toys and encouraging her digging there. This special place will add to Tammy's appreciation of her yard and often will occupy her for hours.

Chewing

Mouthing is Tammy's method of investigating her environment. Her chewing isn't limited to indoor, yummy items. Anything in her reach will be investigated and its taste recorded for future reference. Any item that exercises her strong teeth and jaw muscles will be even more attractive. Objects that can't be removed from her reach can be treated with a distasteful product to discourage her. Nontoxic products

such as Bitter Apple and similar preparations are available in pet supply stores, and may be used inside your home as well.

Keep all doors closed to your garage, garden shed, or other buildings in your backyard. When fertilizing or weed-treating your lawn, make sure the toxic chemicals are watered well into the ground before allowing Tammy access. Sponge up or hose off puddles of chemical-laced water that have pooled on the sidewalk.

Kennel and Run

If you have a fancy backyard, complete with decorative shrubs, young fruit trees, border flowers, and the like, you might consider a separate kennel and run. Regardless of its dimensions, however, don't ever think such a run is a substitute for companionship. Providing the space for exercise isn't the same as taking your Westie for a walk, romping with her, or playing games. A kennel and run allows you to have a backyard party without Tammy getting underfoot. It's also a great place to confine her when workmen are in and about the yard, and at other times.

Note: A run and doghouse should never be used to punish Tammy, or to confine her for hours at a time when your family is home. Westies are family dogs, not objects to be kept behind bars except for convenient times!

Boarding

Sometimes, without warning your family needs to be away; plan for those eventualities. Contact friends and neighbors or relatives and ask them to dog-sit Tammy in your home and yard. A close neighbor is the best choice,

All Westies need toys.

Westies and autumn weather are a perfect match.

providing she likes Tammy and is reliable. Before she's needed, ask her to come to your home and observe your canine duties. Provide full written instructions relative to Tammy's needed exercise, feeding, grooming, and other vital dog-ownership duties. Offer her reasonable compensation, but don't settle for her six-year-old child! Be certain the adult neighbor fully understands that caring for Tammy is an honor and an obligation that should be taken seriously.

Commerical Boarding Facilities

If it is necessary to use a commercial boarding facility, ask Tammy's breeder and your veterinarian to recommend one. Ask the veterinarian if any precautionary measures should be taken to protect Tammy from the stress of boarding.

✔ If necessary, drive across town to use a recommended, well managed, clean boarding kennel. Visit it before it is needed and without warning to assure the cleanliness and quality of its small-dog facilities.

"This is my chair; you sit on the sofa."

A microchip implant is a positive, permanent identification.

which is engraved your name, address, and telephone number. If you have an unlisted number, put it on Tammy's tag anyway. Anyone who finds your Westie must be able to reach her owner.

Microchips: Every Westie should be identified by a subcutaneously implanted microchip containing information about her identity, which will assure her speedy recovery if she lands in "jail." This chip is read with a scanner that's used in practically all shelters and pounds, and most veterinary offices. The microchip only speeds her return to you; it doesn't pay the running-at-large penalty or the costs for repair of her broken leg!

Tattooing: Tattooing is another positive means of identification. A flank or ear tattoo may be a series of letters or numbers that you've recorded with a national registry, or in some cases, owners request their names be used. A veterinarian does tattooing, usually while Tammy is sedated.

Microchips can be implanted by breeders or by your veterinarian on Tammy's first visit. Tattoos usually wait until Tammy has reached the age when sedation is not a risk. Tags should be worn as soon as Tammy routinely is wearing her collar.

✔ Be sure runs are separated by block or brick walls to prevent contact with other dogs.
✔ Inspect the food being fed, bedding used, and escape potential, and meet the kennel staff.
✔ Check the occupied kennels for personal items and find out whether or not you can bring Tammy's bed and toys.

When you deliver Tammy to the kennel, take along a well-worn T-shirt or pair of old socks that haven't been laundered and put them in her kennel. Although this won't ease her loneliness or alleviate all stress, she should realize that you'll soon return for her.

Identification

Purchase a name tag for Tammy before you've collected her from the breeder, or at least on your very first trip to a pet supply store. She eventually should be positively identified by other methods, but the easiest means of identification is a small metal tag on

Crate

Buy a crate before you collect Tammy; a medium-sized fiberglass crate will do nicely. Use her crate to take her home, and put it in

CHECKLIST

Preparation

It's wonderful to be finally getting your Westie. Before bringing home your new bundle of joy, you must make sure that your home is as safe as possible for your new pet.

1 Puppy-proof your entire house. Eliminate hazards before your new pet arrives. Be sure to thoroughly clean and sanitize your pet's living area.

2 Puppy-proof your backyard. Ideally, your entire yard should be completely fenced and escape-proof. Westies are diggers and your fencing should be sturdy enough to contain your pet. Chain-link fencing can be sunk several inches below ground for even greater security.

3 Control chewing. While your Westie puppy is teething, you'll need to keep her and your surroundings protected. Remove anything portable that you wish to safeguard and protect everything else with Bitter Apple or a similar product. Keep any toxic substances out of her reach.

4 A kennel and run is helpful if you don't fence your entire property. However, this convenience is no replacement for regular exercise and should never be used to isolate your Westie from family life. The enclosure should be at least ten feet long, four feet wide, and three feet high.

5 When boarding is needed, enlist the help of a reliable neighbor so your Westie can remain at home. If this is not feasible, use the best boarding kennel you can find. Inspect the kennel in advance for cleanliness and safety.

6 Whenever your Westie is outside your home, she should wear a collar and tag. Many owners have their dogs tattooed with their Social Security numbers, and still others will have their dogs microchipped as a means of permanent identification.

7 Dogs are den animals by nature and will be very comfortable in a crate. This is also an invaluable housebreaking aid, a safe enclosure for travel, and a dog's own place in the home. There are many styles of crates, but you should select one that is versatile, easily cleaned, and large enough for an adult Westie.

the room where she will be spending most of her time. Leave it in a secluded place with its door open and a toy or two inside. It'll keep a tiny puppy out of danger and will become her refuge. Dogs have an instinctive denning behavior: let Tammy exercise it. Crates are also useful for housebreaking, and when you take Tammy on car trips.

By eight weeks of age, Duff is totally familiar with his nest environment. He knows how much rowdiness his dam and siblings will tolerate and he's accustomed to human touch. He has a warm bed, momma to clean and cuddle him, brothers and sisters to wrestle, plenty of good food to eat, and some interesting human faces to lick. It can't get any better. His nest education is complete and he has no idea this good life is coming to an abrupt end.

One day, strange human hands reach down and pluck him from Utopia and the confusion begins. A new voice offers a few soft words and a scented chin snuggles him for a minute, but before he can lick the face, he's placed in a plastic box. He panics when the steel gate snaps, shutting him away from his familiar world. He's frightened, and trembles in a corner until he sniffs a familiar odor. It's just a crumpled towel, but it carries the familiar scent of his mother and siblings. That's better!

His plastic world begins to sway as he's taken to the waiting car. The sudden loud slam of car doors renews his fear and he's panic-stricken again when the roaring engine invades the silence. What has poor Duff done to deserve this fate?

"How did you get up there?"

First Days

Westies' inherent self-confidence enables them to take life's little stresses in stride but Duff's first days in your home are bound to be frightening. Everything's so different in his new environment! He's carried high off the floor, taken outside, and set down in soft earth that he's never before experienced. He's plunked down before a bowl of food but there's no sibling competition. New human faces surround him and one swoops him up immediately after he's eaten. He's passed from one to another, kissed, cuddled, and cooed at; everyone seems to be speaking at once, but he recognizes no familiar voice.

For Duff, the stress of a new environment is inevitable but quite temporary, and can be minimized by some common sense on your part. You've already begun to relieve Duff's stress by bringing him home with the towel that you delivered to the kennel several days ago. You'll leave it in his crate for several days, letting him sleep on it. After a week, you can substitute an article of unwashed clothing from his favorite new human. A T-shirt is okay, but a pair of old socks is better; the smell of familiar feet will comfort him when he's lonely or distressed.

Another stress control is to minimize the greeting crowd. Under your close observation, allow him to investigate his new home. Give him access to first one room, then another. Grant him as much time as needed to search each nook and cranny, and don't be in a hurry to pick him up unless he shows signs of impending defecation or urination. Each time he begins to turn in circles or squat, pluck him from the floor and carry him to his toilet area of the yard (see Housebreaking, page 41).

Diet and Feeding Schedule

When you collect Duff, ask the breeder for a week's supply of his puppy food and maintain his former schedule for that length of time. If he's doing well but you want to improve the food quality, make all changes very slowly (see Westie Nutrition, page 57).

Overeating and gulping his food are dietary stressors you can and should control. Duff may wolf down his food as if he's starved. Don't increase the amount being fed unless he finishes the meal in less than five minutes. If that happens, and he begs for more, wait until the next feeding time and increase the quantity by a small amount. Continue to follow this program until he finishes his meals promptly, then backs off, licks his chops, and acts satisfied. Don't allow vigorous exercise after meals—it's time for a nap.

Building a Lasting Relationship

Bonding is the formation of a permanent, mutually respectful, emotional attachment between the dog and a human. Love and bonding are related but differ slightly and both help to reduce stress. You and your family will demonstrate your love by petting and praise. However, if you are the one who spends the most time instructing Duff, he'll probably quickly bond with you as his mentor.

If you want to be his best friend, be aware that Duff is quite impressionable and eager to follow a leader. Be that leader and immediately take the initiative. It takes time to build a strong bond: playtime, training time, and grooming time. Take time to praise him and give him a treat when he performs well and when you tuck him in his crate at night. Gently but firmly teach him the appropriate behavior in his new capacity. When he begins to *expect* your direction and focuses on your face and hands the bond is strengthened. Soon he'll watch you at every opportunity, twitching his ears and wagging his tail when he hears your voice. Although he may love and obey anyone in the family, he'll be most anxious to please his best friend.

Canine Socialization

Another significant puppy stress relates to meeting new dogs. Canine socialization has been started in his nest but in a single-dog family it needs to be continued. The best way to cope with dog-to-dog stress is to encourage acceptance of other dogs through canine kindergarten. If Duff isn't comfortable and shows signs of timidity or aggressiveness toward other dogs, ask your breeder or veterinarian for the name of a nearby kindergarten class. Under the watchful eyes of an expert dog trainer, he'll be allowed to romp and play with other pups of similar age and size. Usually these classes accept puppies older than 10 or 12 weeks after he's finished his vaccination series.

Human Socialization

Human socialization is acceptance of and compliance with human standards, otherwise known as his manners or the way he treats outsiders who invade his domain. It might be defined as his role and conduct in the presence of strangers.

Acceptance of human standards isn't genetic; it's learned and must be encouraged in as many ways as you can devise. Duff's blending with human society takes a long time to perfect and his training should begin the first day in your home.

Shyness

Shyness is a common manifestation of lack of socialization and to amend this problem, ask an adult friend to visit. Instruct her to move slowly, talk softly, and ignore Duff. She shouldn't insist on holding or petting him, but should allow him to sniff her shoes at his leisure. Perhaps on the second visit, your friend can sit on the floor and pet Duff gently when he approaches. Never allow a stranger to suddenly snatch him up or grasp him tightly. After he's met his visitor several times, she should take a treat from your hand and offer it to him. Repeat this exercise as often as necessary, then introduce another person, then a third.

One child at a time should be the rule. Avoid mobs of children in your home for several weeks, and when they show up unexpectedly, encourage your tiny companion to take refuge in his crate. Westies are tough, but not tough enough to be mauled by a gaggle of noisy kids, at least not until they learn where their den is located.

Correction

Using preventive programs can minimize stress of correction.

✔ Don't allow Duff to mouth your hand but gently remove it from his mouth and hand him a favorite toy.

✔ Teach children to play with tug toys, and when Duff grabs hands, arms, or clothes, instruct them to stand statue-still and offer him a favorite chew toy.

✔ Teach him which toys are his, and play with him only with them, putting children's toys out of his reach.

✔ When he finds something he shouldn't have, your little white whirlwind will be out of sight and in the process of swallowing it in a heartbeat. Discourage all such actions by quickly reclaiming any foreign object he may find, putting it away, and changing the subject. Don't scold, nag, threaten, or shake your finger in his face, and *never* swat him!

✔ Don't allow children to tease Duff by showing him some interesting item, then snatching it away before he can grab it. That game will promote snapping or biting and sooner or later, you'll find the object in his crate in a million pieces—or worse, you'll find half of it and rely on your veterinarian's X ray to show you the remainder.

"What's this green snake doing in my yard?"

Give your Westies plenty of exercise.

Two Westies will entertain each other.

A Westie gives its affection freely.

Remember, a well-mannered Westie is one that has grown up in a well-mannered family where canine and human miscreants aren't tolerated.

Separation Anxiety

Separation anxiety may develop when a puppy isn't given sufficient human and canine socialization, and becomes excessively attached to and dependent on its owner. It's frequently associated with a timid or insecure Westie and he fusses and cries each time the door closes behind you.

When you first recognize this situation don't encourage Duff's dependency with increased attention. Don't respond by trying to reason with him and anthropomorphize. Remember who's leading and who's following. Westies are wonderful pets, but they're still dogs. You're

the leader of Duff's pack; he's not a voting member and you can't establish *equality* between you and your dog.

Don't sympathize and make a fuss over him upon your return. Each absence creates more anxiety and nervousness and you become worried, which worries him. Soon Duff simply can't tolerate being left alone for more than a few minutes and when left behind, he begins to destroy his environment.

This syndrome is a serious behavioral problem often requiring the intervention of a canine behaviorist. At the first signs of excessive dependency, take steps to reverse the course.

✔ Increase his exercise and training sessions.
✔ Implement canine and human socialization training.
✔ Vary your leaving and arriving times.
✔ Ask a friend with whom Duff is acquainted to drop in unexpectedly when you're away.
✔ Give Duff a feeding cube to keep him occupied or a new chew stick each time you're away.
✔ Offer him a treat when you leave but ignore him for a few minutes when you return.
✔ Introduce a playtime immediately before leaving.
✔ Never jiggle your car keys or otherwise signal your departure.
✔ Crate him for varying times while you're at home, and then begin crating him when you're away for short periods (see Crate Training, page 43).
✔ Always reward him for entering the crate, never when he exits. Feed him in the crate occasionally, and always place something with your scent in the crate.

If these changes aren't effective, consult a behaviorist.

TIP

Off to a Good Start

The first few days in a new home can be stressful both for a Westie puppy and the human members of his new family. Bring home a toy or towel from the breeder that bears the scent of the puppy's birth home. When you put him to bed for the first few nights, that article will serve to comfort him while he is becoming accustomed to his new surroundings. An old-fashioned alarm clock (if you can find one) with a loud tick that mimics the heartbeats of mother and littermates may save you from the lonely cries that are so much a part of having a new puppy in the home.

CHECKLIST

Stress Management

Your new puppy can be subjected to as much stress as you are. If you know how to minimize stress for your Westie companion, you will improve your life and his.

1 A puppy will be frightened by abrupt changes connected to a new home. Articles bearing the scent of his birth home ease the transition slightly, but the adjustment is still a big one. Proceed slowly and soon his natural self-confidence will kick in.

2 Ask the breeder for a small supply of the food your new puppy has been eating. This gives you time to purchase your own supply or acclimate the puppy to another diet. This is also the time you learn, by watching, his eating habits.

3 When a puppy becomes comfortable in his new home he will begin to bond with those around him. A Westie relates well to the whole family, but will usually be closest to the person who spends the most time with him.

4 If your puppy is to be your only dog, consider enrolling him in a canine kindergarten. These classes are wonderful for correcting temperament problems and are worthwhile for all puppies. Ask your veterinarian or breeder about a local class.

5 A puppy properly socialized to people will grow into a dog that will always be a pleasure to live with. Establish his rules of behavior early and stick with them. Your puppy looks to you for the guidance and stability to keep him happy.

6 Administer correction consistently and fairly. Usually your tone of voice is enough for him to get the message. Show the puppy what you expect of him and he should soon respond accordingly. Never tease him or resort to any physical punishment.

7 There will always be times when you cannot be with your puppy, times he must reliably remain alone. He should deal with separation confident in the knowledge that all is well and you will return to him as soon as you can.

WESTIE PRIMARY EDUCATION

Tammy's inherent intelligence, people-pleasing attitude, and talents must be joined with real-life experiences to produce a great pet. The object of her primary education is to mold her many attributes to complement human ideas of acceptable behavior.

Housebreaking

You anticipate with pleasure and anxiety Tammy's first days and nights in your home, then reality gallops in and you wonder whether or not Tammy is worth all the trouble. Full of fun, high spirited, and into everything, Tammy gambols about clumsily and follows you every-where, rarely roaming more than a few yards from you. She'll expect you to respond to her every need including food, water, exercise, play, warm bed, comfort, and praise.

Housebreaking should begin as soon as Tammy arrives in your home.

✔ Introduce her to the designated toilet area in your backyard, and carry her to that exact spot the first thing in the morning, just before bedtime at night, after each feeding, and any-time she begins to circle and sniff the floor. If she's crated at times during the day, she should be taken to the toilet area immediately before

"I smell a varmint down there."

she's confined and directly after she's taken from the crate.

✔ Remove her food and water about two hours before retiring at night and take her for a short backyard walk, followed by a trip to the toilet area, just before you put her to bed.

✔ Step back and be silent while she's in the toilet spot. After she's done her duty, reward her performance with your praise and race her to the back door or toss her favorite toy a few times. If she shows no interest in relieving her-self, wait several minutes, silently pick her up, and return to the house without comment. Remember to reward her *positive* action and ignore the *negative*.

✔ Confine Tammy to a crate, X-pen, or small, easily cleaned room at night. Keep her in a place that isn't big enough for her to defecate and sleep in. If she fusses and cries when she is crated, train yourself to get out of bed and carry her to the toilet area of the yard. Praise her if she performs, but don't scold her if she just sits there looking at you or frisks about. Be patient and silently remain for several minutes, then carry her back to her confinement without grumbling. All this trouble will pay off in a few days or weeks.

Paper Training

Tammy can be paper-trained but it's more trouble and work than teaching her to go outside to a toilet area.

✔ Set up the X-pen in a low-traffic, easily disinfected area of the house.

✔ Cover the entire floor of the pen with a dozen layers of newspaper and when she's not with you, confine her to the pen. Put her bed and water bowl at one end of the pen and she'll probably use the other end for her fecal and urinary deposits.

✔ Pick up her stools and wet papers immediately when found.

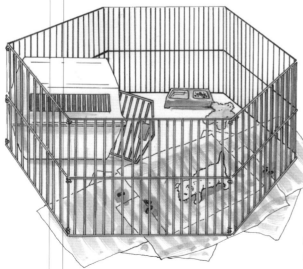

✔ After a week, remove the papers from the bed end of the pen and leave a square of papers at the other. A couple of weeks later leave the gate open. If Tammy returns to the papers to urinate and defecate, you can probably remove the pen and leave the papers in place.

Once paper-trained, it's possible to teach Tammy to go outside for her elimination duties. Simply move the targeted papers a couple of feet a day until they reach the back door. Then pull more and more of the papers under the door, until those remaining inside are too small to hit. Tammy will probably scratch or whine to get outside to the papers, and it's all downhill from there.

Understandable Cues

When you've decided what task you want to teach Tammy, take her to an isolated spot that's devoid of people and away from all distractions. Each teaching session should take no more

If your Westie puppy is to be alone all day, an exercise pen is absolutely necessary.

than five minutes, but can be repeated three or four times daily. Each cue or command should be presented using a particular voice intonation and manner, and a word she understands. Consistency is critically important! Hand signals can be taught without voice commands, but initially the cue should include a verbal command with or without an accompanying hand signal.

For example, if you're teaching Tammy to come, snap a long cord to her collar and

✔ Say her name in a specific, recognizable tone that's neither loud nor gruff, but with timbre and inflection that differs from your normal voice. Hesitate a few seconds to allow the command to soak in.

✔ In the same tone, give the command *"Come"* (accompanied by your hand signal).

✔ If necessary, encourage her to respond by applying light pressure to the cord.

✔ Upon her arrival at your feet tell her *"Good dog"* and offer her a treat.

✔ Give her a release command that's pronounced in the same special tone, *"Okay, Tammy."*

✔ Scratch her ears, pet and praise her, and let her frisk about.

The trick is to take advantage of opportunities; choose your training methods to meet your objectives without letting your student know what you're up to. Imply that she's the smartest dog in the world, never give her a command that she can't obey, and finish each teaching session with a cue she knows well, so you can truthfully commend her. She'll appreciate your praise and will try harder to please you. Establish verbal or physical contact whenever possible; keep her focus centered on you and success will surely follow.

Crate Training

A crate is a nice addition to the décor of any home and it serves several useful purposes. It assists in your housebreaking chores and is a mobile den that helps you protect Tammy from danger. It's her refuge from screaming children, the noise of the TV or surround-sound, or the confusion of a boisterous party.

Your Westie can be confined to her den when you're serving tea and really don't need her help but it's not a penalty box. It's not the place where you ban poor Tammy when she doesn't behave. A crate can be misused and may contribute to abuse! Never toss her in the crate when she's been in mischief or otherwise has earned your displeasure.

Teach Tammy the *crate* command early in her life. Entice her into the crate with a nylon bone and perhaps a rawhide chewy or a feeding cube, and always put something with your scent inside as well. Pet and praise her as she enters, snap the door closed, and leave the area quickly, before she's finished smelling all the goodies you've left.

A few minutes or half an hour later, go to the crate, open the door, and allow her to leave, but don't reward her at this time. Teach her that entering her den is a wonderful treat but leaving it is just another daily event.

Collars and Leashes

You'll probably buy Tammy's puppy collar on your first trip to the pet supply shop. Buckle it on her the first day or two only while you're with her. She'll scratch at it and try to get out of it but if you divert her attention, she'll soon be used to wearing it. Tie a shoelace or a short piece of nylon cord to the collar once she's

become accustomed to its feel around her neck. Let the cord drag behind her while you're with her. She may chase it, run sideways, or glance back at it and act frightened, but that's only temporary.

Walks on leash teach canine socialization.

"Is this the right place to put it?"

After she ignores the dragging cord, or better yet, from the beginning, pick up the loose end and follow her. Every now and then, stop and say, *"Tammy, whoa"* and let the cord tighten. She'll immediately turn toward you and try to back away, but you're prepared and have a treat in your pocket. Drop to one knee and extend the treat, telling her *"Tammy, come."* She obeys, you praise her, give her the treat, and start all over again. She'll begin following or frequently looking back at you, watching for a treat. Practice this exercise frequently for a week or two, sometimes leading, sometimes following. Soon, when she sees you with the leash she'll come to you anxiously, waiting for the walk and the treats in your pocket.

Training Collars

Probably you'll find that a nylon training collar is best when Tammy's a little older and you begin training in earnest. Training collars are misnamed "choke collars," but properly positioned and used, the collar doesn't choke the dog. It applies intermittent pressure, discouraging her from pulling against the leash. If the idea of a choke collar bothers you, try using her buckle collar or a two-piece slip collar, both of which will give you control but apply less pressure over her larynx. No two dogs are alike, and there is no general rule dictating what type of collar you must use.

Leashes

Leashes likewise come in various types, weights, and lengths. Pick a lightweight, 6-foot (1.8-m) nylon lead and buy a 20-foot (6.1-m) lightweight cord for other training, and a retractable lead for use on walks.

After Tammy's been vaccinated, substitute the retractable lead for the cord and take her for a walk around the block or in the park. Make your first excursions short, and continue to encourage her to listen to your voice, watch your actions, and respond to your commands, but don't make each walk a boot camp training course. When it's safe, let her frolic about and sniff all the interesting odors she encounters. For her this is great fun and she'll be more apt to listen closely to you if she's given some liberty part of the time. No matter how obedient Tammy seems, don't trust her off lead! Puppies have remarkably short attention spans, and Tammy will conveniently forget your commands when you least expect it.

Commands

Come

Some early lessons overlap others. For example, Tammy will be taught her name during the first few days in your home.

1. When you speak her name and she starts toward you, immediately tell her *"Come."*

2. When she responds, reward her with your praise and a scratch.

3. If she ignores the *come* command, don't repeat it immediately. Wait a few minutes, drop to one knee, pat the ground, and say, *"Tammy, come."* She can't resist this offered affection and will respond quickly.

4. When she arrives, pet and make a fuss over her, and tell her how clever she is.

Take advantage of every tool. When you've prepared her food, sneak into the backyard and

"What's with all the sitting stuff? I'm just a baby!"

say, *"Tammy, come."* When she looks up, show her her dish. When she arrives at your feet, first reward her with your praise, then give her her food. In this way you'll teach her name, the *come* command, and reward each response.

To reinforce the *come* command, tie the long training cord to her collar and allow her to wander off a dozen yards. Drop to one knee, and call her name. When she looks up, say in your command voice, *"Tammy, come."* Don't repeat the cue! If she doesn't respond immediately, hastily reel her in until she's at your side or on your lap. Upon her arrival, tell her she's a fine dog, praise her, give her a little treat, and let her wander off again. Continue to reinforce the *come* command as frequently as necessary.

Sit

1. Place Tammy in a standing position in front of you and put a small treat in your hand.

2. When you have her attention tell her, *"Tammy, sit."* Hesitate for a few seconds, then show her the treat just above her muzzle and move it slowly backward over her head. She'll almost certainly plant her bottom on the grass. If she doesn't, apply slight pressure on her rump with your other hand.

3. When she sits, praise her, release her with the *okay* command, and give her more verbal praise and the treat.

Stay

This exercise is quite difficult for immature puppies to learn but it should be taught when she's mastered *"Sit"* on command.

1. When Tammy obeys you and is sitting, in your special voice give her the cue *"Stay,"* and show her the palm of your hand a few inches in front of her face.

2. Hold your hand there until she's sat for several seconds, then release, treat, and praise her.

3. *Stay* can be gradually lengthened and eventually you should be able to back away several feet while she remains sitting.

Down

This task is taught and sometimes used together with the sit command or by itself.

1. *Down* means that Tammy is to position her belly flat on the ground.

2. After she's given the *down* command, move the treat lower in front of her till it's against the ground, and if necessary, apply slight downward hand pressure on her withers.

3. *Down* can be combined with *stay* as discussed above.

Heel

"Heel" means to walk with her nose exactly even with your left knee, at your pace, when you turn, turn about, speed up, slow down, or stop. In an obedience trial, various exercises are accomplished in an arena together with other dogs and handlers. That's a lot to ask of a Westie puppy, but you can teach Tammy to heel if you first pave the way with simple training. Teaching *"heel"* requires a maximum focus on you, your actions, your gait, and your hands. Subtle cues are given with her leash, and later her focus on you will be sufficient. If you propose to follow obedience work seriously, join an obedience club. Only in such an arena with a reputable trainer's advice should you work with such commands.

Walk On

This cue is used to encourage Tammy to get on with your walk, leave the most recent scent behind, and forget about the chipmunk across the fence in the hollow log. It's taught by tossing a small biscuit or her favorite toy ahead of you on the trail and simultaneously giving the *walk on* command. If Tammy's more interested in the varmint than the toy or biscuit, pick her up and restart her a few yards down the trail. The point is, don't tug her leash and drag her along behind. Instead, encourage a new direction by substituting something else for the unattainable and change her point of interest.

Constructive Exercise

Providing the place for exercise is not the same as participating in it. An empty, boring backyard won't work forever and sooner or later, she'll rebel when left alone. To truly appreciate Tammy, take her for leashed walks, especially where she'll meet other animals. Her walks out of the yard should begin as soon as she's finished her puppy vaccination series.

Walks need not be overly long, but as she reaches adolescence and maturity the journeys can be increased.

Exercise is your goal but remember Tammy's instincts must be satisfied. Her focus on your commands, training she's received, and games you've played with her in the yard will all be remembered, but hereditary drives and urges will surface in an adolescent Westie.

Fences and leashes always control Tammy, but obedience training is a little less predictable. You've spent hours teaching her to *whoa* and *come*. She's perfect in her backyard, but exercises taught there are really only a Westie's method of training the teacher. She'll lure you into complacency and let you believe her obedient response is quick and absolute. You snap off the leash, about the time she spies an unwary chipmunk, and instantly, the old terrier instinct leaps forward and she's off!

Fun and Games at Home

These games follow no particular pattern; use whatever technique you can devise to encourage Tammy's interest. Try to increase the challenge level of each game as she matures; Westies are problem solvers and need challenges.

Find

While she's watching, hide a treat under a throw rug and tell her to *"Find."* Naturally she'll race to the rug, burrow under it, and gobble up the treat. After a few such finds, a friend can hold Tammy while you drag the treat along the floor on a string, then hide it behind a door or other easily accessible place in another room. Carry this game outside in fair weather, and let Tammy find the treats hidden behind trees, buried under an inch of sand.

Fetch

Teach Tammy to fetch by showing her a ball that's too large to swallow. Toss the ball while holding her collar. Tell her, *"Fetch,"* and release her. Most Westies are ball crazy, so she'll probably run directly to the ball, but she'll likely grab it and take it for a run around the yard.

Fetch has an implied meaning of returning the object to you. If you want her to bring it to you, fasten the long lead to her collar before you begin. Toss the ball, give the *fetch* command, and let the line feed out. Then encourage her to return to you by giving the *come* command and reeling in the line. When she arrives before you, give her the *sit* command and offer her a treat while she still holds the ball. She'll release the ball into your hand to get the treat, and you've taught her to fetch.

Learned Behavior Versus Instinctive Traits

Regardless of Tammy's age or the amount of training you've done with her, remember that inappropriate behavior is also learned and can be altered with persistence and patience. Approach the problem behavior with a positive attitude. Don't expect miracles or overnight obedience, but it can be modified if you take the time and have the knowledge to properly alter it.

Establish a reward, one for which Tammy will always respond. It might be an edible treat or a word of praise, and give it immediately and consistently when she responds.

WESTIE GROOMING

Grooming includes general bodily care. On your first visit to Duff's veterinarian, ask the clinician to show you how to examine him for abnormalities that you should watch for, including his skin, feet, eyes, mouth, nose, and weight or condition. Take notes, and mark your calendar each time you groom him.

The Westie is a high-maintenance breed. Duff should be brushed briskly using a medium slicker, two or three times a week even if you like the scruffy look, and professionally groomed three times a year. Westies have a predisposition to skin disease, which may be worsened by improper grooming, too much bathing, or using an inappropriate shampoo. If you suspect a skin disease, seek a professional diagnosis and continue therapy until you are told to stop.

To Bathe or Not to Bathe

Duff's first act in your backyard is to find a mud puddle and play in it and your immediate impulse is to bathe him. Hold that thought! It might be better to blot his coat with a towel, let it dry thoroughly, and brush out the dirt. You'll be surprised at how white his coat is after brushing.

As a tiny puppy, Duff can rather easily suffer from hypothermia (loss of body heat) and should not be routinely bathed unless really

"Hey, I like this!"

necessary until he's older, stronger, and has more resistance. Don't add the stress of a bath to that already present because of environmental changes and his adjustment to a new human pack. However, combing and brushing are excellent ways to bond with a young Westie and keep him clean in the bargain.

If it's necessary to bathe him, use a logical approach and Duff should suffer no ill effects.

1. Be sure the room is warm and free of drafts. Use the sprayer hose that's found on many kitchen sinks, and if one isn't available, buy a rubber sprayer hose that fits over the faucet nozzle.

2. Put a rubber mat in the bottom of the sink to prevent slipping.

3. Warm a couple of towels in the clothes dryer and stack them on the chair behind you together with your hand-held hair dryer.

4. Place Duff in the sink with a few inches of tepid water in the bottom. Except for his head, soak his coat with warm water by holding the sprayer close to his skin.

5. Lather his coat well with a mild shampoo designed for dogs. Human shampoos with an acid pH of 5.5 should not be used on a Westie's skin that has an alkaline pH of 7.5.

6. After soaping, rinse his coat thoroughly with warm water by holding the sprayer against his skin, then towel him as dry as possible.

7. Finish drying Duff's coat with your hand-held hair dryer set on the lowest warm setting, holding it several inches from his body, and lightly brushing his coat away from his skin. His face, ears, and muzzle should be wiped clean with a damp washcloth and dried with a warm towel. Don't spray water or direct the dryer toward his face, including ears or eyes.

Westies don't shed heavily and rarely develop a doggy odor; therefore, you can bathe Duff only when absolutely necessary until he's about a year old. After that he can be bathed when he finds something nasty to play in while on a walk, or when he roots in mud or dirt. Under normal circumstances, you'll find that his coat can be kept quite clean with frequent combing and brushing.

When the bathing program is finished, keep him inside for several hours to be sure he's

---

TIP

Before the Bath

Before bathing Duff as an adult, clean his ears with your finger wrapped with gauze that has been dampened with alcohol. After cleaning, plug his ear canals with twisted cotton balls. Then apply a mild ophthalmic ointment in each eye. Now bathe as described above and you can carefully lather his head without danger.

---

totally dry before he flies around the yard and rolls in garden dirt or something worse.

Skin and Coat Care

Examine Duff's skin carefully about once a week. If he scratches indiscriminately or develops red, irritated skin lesions take him to his veterinarian. Don't diagnose the problem at home, and don't give him a flea, tick, or mange bath with medicated shampoo! No medicated shampoo is universally beneficial, and generally, medicated baths are contraindicated unless prescribed by your veterinarian.

Duff's outer guard hair is dry, hard, and stiff, and is about 2 inches (5.1 cm) long when he reaches adulthood. The undercoat is shorter, thicker, and softer. Its normal dryness makes his coat easy to care for unless he is destined for conformation shows. Preparing a Westie for judging is an art, one that takes years of patient practice to learn. The breed standard states that the West Highland White Terrier's coat is "very important and seldom seen to perfection." This should clue you to seek professional grooming help and advice if you and Duff are embarking on a show career. Most dog groomers lack the knowledge necessary to groom a Westie for the show ring. Ask a Westie breeder or an experienced Westie handler to teach you the proper method of plucking his coat for exhibition. Hair is plucked to give his head a roundish appearance and that over his neck and shoulders is plucked or trimmed to blend with his body hair, abdominal covering, and leg furnishings. With proper instruction, you can do this at home and may find it enjoyable. However, frequent clipping with scissors or electric clippers will encourage a softer, silkier, fluffier regrowth that is scorned by serious Westie fanciers.

Many pet Westies are simply left natural or clipped by dog groomers who can shorten Duff's coat and trim his feet. You'll probably think he looks grand, and well he might!

Teeth

As soon as Duff is well established in your home and while he is still young enough to be easily influenced, begin a regular teeth-brushing program. Buy any one of several canine toothbrushes and a tube of canine toothpaste, and start brushing his teeth at least once a week. As he matures, he'll accept this program readily if it's associated with a regular playtime or before a walk.

Watch for double teeth at about three months of age (see Double Dentition, page 72). As he matures, check regularly for broken teeth, foreign material, gingival (gum) wounds, gum redness, halitosis, and tartar buildup. At four or five years, he may require annual tartar scaling by your veterinarian. Sometimes this is done without sedation, but usually a short-term anesthetic is required. Broken teeth are usually extracted if the fracture extends below the gum line. Teeth implants are occasionally set to take the place of an extracted tooth, but this is your prerogative. Consult your veterinarian.

Feet and Nails

Weekly grooming includes Duff's feet and toenails. Examine his pads for injuries, look between his toes for tangled hair or burrs, and check the length of his nails. If the nails are excessively long, split, or broken, reach for the clippers. Check all of his nail lengths and don't forget his dewclaws, which correspond to our thumbs.

Either a guillotine or scissor-type nail clipper will do a good job if sharp and properly used. Although it's unlikely that a serious injury or infection will result from nail clipping, try not to cut any too short. Be prepared and have on hand a styptic pencil or some coagulant such as silver nitrate. Clip off only the sharp tip of each nail every week while Duff's still a puppy and when he really needs a pedicure he'll have more confidence in your technique. If you're unsure of your technique, have a professional teach you so that you don't hurt Duff.

If nail care has been neglected, select a long nail and nip off the sharp tip. You'll see that the nail cross section resembles an upside down V. Make consecutive thin slices until the nail is softer and cross sections of the nail pieces are formed like a circle with a notch in the bottom instead of a V. That's far enough! If you cut a nail too short, several things will happen: Duff will whine or yip, the nail's vascular bed will bleed, and he will undoubtedly be harder to catch the next time you reach for the clippers.

If you discover a broken nail that's tender and seeping blood, or if you create that problem with your nail trimmers, hold Duff's foot securely and press against the bleeding nail a styptic pencil or a silver nitrate stick that's available from pet supply shops. Hold the coagulant tightly in place for about three minutes and release. If blood continues to seep after a couple of applications, bandage the foot snuggly but not tight enough to stop circulation in the foot. Leave the bandage on for eight hours, and restrict his exercise for a few days.

"Be careful back there, buddy."

"Me? Need a bath? No way."

Chew toys are good for the teeth.

"You call for help and I'll sit tight."

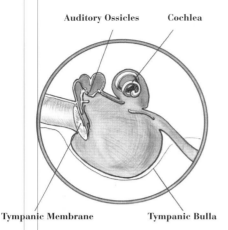

Auditory Ossicles   Cochlea

Tympanic Membrane   Tympanic Bulla

Internal anatomy of the ear.

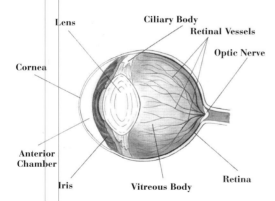

Lens   Ciliary Body

Retinal Vessels

Optic Nerve

Cornea

Anterior Chamber

Iris   Vitreous Body   Retina

Anatomy of the eye.

Ears

During weekly grooming sessions, check Duff's ears. Don't poke cotton swabs into his ear canals, but instead look closely into the canals for dark wax. If wax is abundant, wrap your index finger with gauze dampened with alcohol and clean the canals. If his ear canals smell foul or exude excessive wax, make an appointment with your veterinarian for examination. Abnormal head carriage is another sign of otitis (ear canal inflammation). If he tips his head to the side, shakes, or scratches his ears, consult a veterinarian.

Eyes

A Westie's dark eyes should appear bright, shiny, and clean. Excessive tearing, greenish yellow pus, or any appreciable discharge exuding from them is abnormal. Check his conjunctiva, which is the mucous membrane that lines the eyelids. If it's red or appears irritated, or if the blood vessels are enlarged, conjunctivitis may be present. Examine his cornea, which is the front, clear part of the eyeball. The cornea should always be clear as glass, bright, and shiny. If any abnormalities are seen, consult your veterinarian.

CHECKLIST

Grooming

When your Westie looks good, he feels good, and you can take pride in his appearance. It takes some practice and effort to groom well, but it's worth the effort and it's fun too.

1 Bathe your Westie only when necessary. Regularly scheduled brushing and combing are usually enough to keep him clean and attractive. When you must bathe him, stand him on a non-slip mat, use a mild shampoo, and work in a warm, draft-free room.

2 A healthy skin is essential to a healthy coat. Check your Westie's skin every time you groom him and take him to your veterinarian as soon as possible if he appears to scratch excessively or if you notice any irritation or redness.

3 Begin a regularly scheduled program of tooth brushing while he is a puppy, and your Westie's teeth should remain strong and healthy for life. Dental scaling performed by your veterinarian may become an annual necessity when your dog reaches middle age.

4 Always check your dog's feet during each grooming session. Look between the toes for any redness or foreign objects and injuries to the pads. Remove a small portion of each nail every time and you lower the risk of injury. Don't forget the dewclaws.

5 Check inside your dog's ears whenever you groom him and wipe them gently with alcohol on a cotton ball. If you notice an offensive odor, excessive wax or hair, or he carries his head to the side, take him to your veterinarian.

6 There can be no mistaking healthy eyes in a Westie. They are typically bright and clear and there will be no excessive matter present. If you notice any redness around the eyelids, or an unusual volume of matter or tears, tell your veterinarian.

WESTIE NUTRITION

In addition to the proper kind and quantity of food, fresh clean drinking water is necessary for life. Invest in several stainless steel bowls for Tammy's food and water and wash them daily in hot, soapy water.

Feeding Your Westie

Feed Tammy exactly as her breeder indicated. Use the same food, given at the same frequency and in the same quantities for at least a week. After she's accustomed to her new environment, you can gradually increase quantities or make brand changes if necessary. Mix one-quarter new food, three-quarters old food for several days, then one-half new, and one-half old, and so forth.

Premium quality food isn't expensive because it furnishes Tammy with balanced nutrition, is palatable, highly digestible, and is packaged in small quantities to insure freshness. If you have a problem with the breeder's food and you wish to change, buy a premium dry puppy ration and add a little warm water or fat-free broth to soften the dry food.

Frequency

Growing puppies require twice the calories of adults, and small active breeds require more calories per pound of body weight than big

"I wish they would come home."

breeds. This tells you that a Westie puppy is at the top of that pyramid.

Divide Tammy's daily puppy ration into three meals daily until she's six months old and two daily from six months to a year. At a year, her diet can be changed to an adult ration of equal quality, fed once daily, but she'll be happier with two meals a day permanently.

During intensive training periods or other times of activity or stress, increase the quantities of food in each meal. Weigh Tammy weekly while she's a growing puppy, and anytime she's training or working. If she fails to maintain her growth rate or if she loses weight, increase the quantity of each meal slightly until her weight stabilizes. If she begins to look pudgy and her weight is climbing, decrease the quantity of her food until her weight remains constant. Each time she's weighed, record her weight and the quantity being fed.

Tammy's physical fitness can be estimated by her weight, the feel of her ribs, and monitoring her energy level. If her ribs are palpable under a thin layer of fat, her skin is supple and moves easily across her ribs, and she's always ready to go, she's probably in top shape.

Dog Food Labels

Labels are legal documents that tell you a great deal, but only if fully understood. A label identifies the ingredients, which are listed in the order of quantity. If soy flour is listed first, the product contains more soy flour than any other ingredient. Certain labels reveal that the food meets the requirements of the National Research Council, but that statement may apply only to *maintenance* requirements. In other words, the food is adequate for dogs under minimal stress, but is insufficient for growing puppies, performance, or breeding dogs. The bioavailability is the percent of an ingredient that is metabolized by the dog. If a label specifies the total quantity of an element, but doesn't mention its *bioavailability,* you've learned nothing.

Calories

Kcal (kilocalorie) is the amount of energy produced from a food element when it's digested by Tammy's body. Technically, 1 Kcal is the amount of heat energy required to bring 1 kg of water from 50 to 61°F (15 to 16°C).

Fat

Fat contains 9 Kcal per gram and is a calorie-dense nutrient containing all required fatty acids. Animal fat tastes better than vegetable fat, but both types provide adequate fatty acids for your Westie. Adult maintenance diets should contain at least 5 percent fat. Slightly more may be desirable to improve coat quality or palatability, but remember that in excess, fat is dangerous.

Protein Quality and Quantity

Vegetable proteins have slightly lower bioavailability and less palatability and are said to be lower quality than animal proteins. Adult maintenance diets should contain about 18 percent protein, including specific amounts of 10 essential amino acids. Amino acid deficiency may result in poor coat, reduced growth rate, and weight loss.

Generally, 20 percent dietary protein is sufficient for growing puppies, but 15 percent or less is too little. Training increases protein demand, and aging decreases demand. As a senior Westie, Tammy will require a lower quantity of protein of a higher quality.

Carbohydrates

Calories obtained from carbohydrates or starch often are the cause of obesity. Dogs have an almost insignificant requirement for starch, but some manufacturers use this inexpensive element to increase their food's caloric content.

Minerals

Twelve essential minerals are required for canine life, including a ratio of 1.2 to 1.4 parts calcium to 1 part phosphorus.

Vitamins

Eleven vitamins are essential in canine diets. Vitamin C isn't required because dogs adequately manufacture it. Vitamin A can be toxic in high doses, and the requirements for vitamins D and E are interrelated with other nutrients.

Types of Food

Canned Food

Canned food is expensive and quite palatable but it may not give Tammy adequate fiber in her diet. It may predispose her to urinary frequency caused by preservatives and seasoning, and because it contains more than 50 percent water. Meat quality in some canned food isn't the best and some canned foods are laced with colored soy products but virtually no meat.

Semimoist or Soft-Moist

Soft-moist dog food looks like ground meat, but it rarely contains any appreciable quantity of animal protein. It costs more per pound than either dry or canned food, and may contain sugars and chemical preservatives that add health risks. Semimoist products can promote excessive drinking and frequent urination, and are sometimes incriminated as the cause for allergic reactions.

Kibble

Kibble (dry dog food) usually is the least expensive and best diet for Tammy but all dry foods aren't equal. They are as different as the dogs that eat them, varying in cost, quality, and palatability.

Premium Foods

Premium foods are pricey, but biologically the most economical. You'll feed a smaller quantity because high bioavailability or quality also means smaller volumes of feces. If necessary, palatability may be improved by mixing premium dry foods with similar premium canned products.

Brand Name Products

Brand name kibble has been around for many years and often provides excellent nutrition. If in doubt about its quality, call or write to the manufacturer and ask for the bioavailability of each element, feeding trial results, analysis, and the sources of the ingredients.

Generic Brands

Ingredients' seasonal variation causes problems in generics because supply and demand govern the cereal products used in generic formulation. If wheat is plentiful, you may find it higher in the formula, and a bumper corn crop will increase the quantities of that grain.

Puppy Rations

Puppy foods are specifically formulated to furnish adequate nutritional balance for

---

TIP

Special Diets

Dog owners today are fortunate to have a variety of scientifically balanced, complete foods in both canned and dry formulations available to them for pets with special health needs. If your dog is overweight, has heart or kidney problems, or is suffering from a food allergy, your veterinarian may recommend that you put your dog on such a diet. Some special needs diets are available only through a veterinarian, while others can be purchased from a pet food dealer. If your dog's health would benefit from one of these diets and your veterinarian agrees, you should put her on it as soon as possible, both to improve her quality of life and to extend her life well into her senior years. As with all diet changes, make the transition gradual in order to avoid any intestinal upsets.

"Good thing I got a coat for Christmas."

Three youngsters in search of adventure.

"I know you're in there."

"I smell a chipmunk in here somewhere."

Most Westies are enthusiastic eaters.

CHECKLIST

Nutrition

The typical Westie is an enthusiastic eater and will thrive on any good diet. Feed her a balanced ration at the same time every day and make sure she doesn't overdo.

1 Keep a new puppy on the diet she ate before you got her, making any changes gradually. Feed in the same place and at the same time daily. The proof of a good diet is the energy and condition of the dog that eats it.

2 Commercial dog food is available in many forms. Compare the various types and brands and ask your breeder and veterinarian what they advise. When considering a dog food, remember that the ads are meant to appeal to you—not your pet.

3 Puppy rations are formulated for a specific stage in the dog's life cycle. As with formulations for adult dogs, some brands are better than others are. Gather some expert advice and learn to read puppy food labels to find the right one for your pet.

4 Westies love to chew, so be sure to give your pet only safe chew items. Food treats should be given sparingly and never as a substitute for the normal diet. Just as with her main diet, select quality treat items, not doggy "junk food."

5 Supplements may seem like a good idea, but a balanced diet should give your pet all the nutrition she needs. Dogs recovering from illness or in high stress situations may need supplements. Seek your veterinarian's advice before using one of these.

6 Your Westie will probably try to wheedle some of whatever you eat. However, it is best to keep her and human food a safe distance apart. There are too many kinds of food that can be upsetting or—like chocolate—even dangerous.

growth and development of young dogs. As in other foods, you'll get what you pay for. Quality, sources, and bioavailability of constituents vary. Feeding trials also are performed on puppy foods, and constituent identification labels are found on them as well.

Consumable Chewies and Treats

Chewies formed by pressing tiny bits of rawhide into sticks generally are quite safe, but those composed of single, large, twisted chunks of rawhide may cause digestive blockage problems. Pigs' ears and snouts and other similar pieces of hardened animal cartilage or hide should be avoided.

Small dogs get small treats. Treats are fine for training rewards if Tammy doesn't receive more than a tablespoonful or two daily. Use a small amount of her regular dog food for a reward if she responds well to that. Reward her—don't overfeed her. Measure the quantity of her treats and deduct that amount from her daily ration. When buying treats, check the ingredients the same as you would her regular food.

Supplements

Don't arbitrarily feed vitamin-mineral or fat supplements. Your veterinarian may prescribe vegetable or fish oil, lecithin, or fatty acid products to aid in the treatment of skin disease, but Tammy's total diet should be considered and modified to maintain proper balance. Ask a veterinarian about stress supplements and always check before using over-the-counter supplements.

Human Food

Keep human foods off the floor and out of reach.
✔ Milk can bring on bouts of diarrhea.
✔ Meats *may* cause diarrhea and *will* upset nutritional balance.
✔ Bones, especially chicken or chop bones, ribs, and steak and roast bones may splinter

TIP

Homemade Diets

Formulating Tammy's diet in your kitchen can lead to many problems. Leave dog food production to those who have analytical laboratories, research facilities, and feeding trials to test their products.

and bone shards may puncture her mouth or throat or, if swallowed, they can cause other digestive problems.
✔ Ice cream, candy, pizza, potato chips, peanuts, and many other human junk foods often are difficult to digest and should never be fed.

When fed regularly, when contaminated, or when excessively rich, table scraps can cause damage to canine pancreatic ducts and if not treated adequately, can have fatal results. Generally, feeding table scraps should be avoided.

Warning: Chocolate can poison your dog.

If you've accepted responsibility for Duff, you should take charge of his health care and plan for success by establishing a health enhancement scheme that includes preventive measures as well as prompt attention to emergencies.

The Veterinarian

Before Duff requires the services of a veterinarian, consider your choice of a veterinary clinician. Obtain referrals from your breeder and talk to neighbors, then call for a well-dog appointment with a community practitioner.

On your first visit, introduce yourself and Duff and tell the veterinarian that you're shopping for health care. Look at the equipment being used and notice if it's modern, clean, and appears well maintained. Inquire about fees for specific services such as vaccinations, spaying, and routine office calls. Ask to tour the animal hospital and notice if it's clean and well kept. Ask how out-of-hours emergencies are handled and if they are referred to other facilities, ask to tour them as well. If your findings aren't to your liking, seek another veterinarian!

Preventive Care

Establish a regular home examination.
✔ At least once a month set Duff on a sturdy table and examine his ears for excessive wax and bad odors.

Outdoor forays are favorite diversions.

✔ Check his teeth and mucous membranes of his mouth and throat for injuries or foreign material caught between teeth.
✔ Inspect his eyes for redness, discharge, and irritation.
✔ Examine his feet, including hair, pads, toes, nails, and dewclaws.
✔ Feel his ribs, then weigh him on your bathroom scale, just to be sure he's not losing or gaining weight.
✔ Check his anus and genitalia for excessive redness, pus, and matted hair.
✔ Feel each leg joint and make note of any that are tender when touched.

When the examination is completed mark on a calendar the date and your findings. Your routine examination findings will be quite important if Duff contracts a disease. At least once a year, schedule an appointment for a veterinary well-dog examination and booster vaccination.

Vaccinations

General immunization schedules are a thing of the past because certain diseases are more prevalent in some areas than others and no two dogs are identical. Disease exposure potential is different for each individual. Some vaccines confer longer immunity than others, causing some veterinarians to base their immunization program on blood tests, but unfortunately the tests often cost a great deal more than a combination booster vaccination. Adverse tissue reactions occur when certain vaccines are used in some individuals, which has led to formulation of an immunization schedule that addresses each individual puppy as well as the safety and effectiveness of each individual vaccine.

Don't accept yesterday's advice that all puppies of all breeds need one series of vaccinations at a certain age, and another multivalent vaccine at preselected intervals. You must examine the cost of possibly unnecessary vaccines and the risks involved with their administration. The choice of a multiple-type booster or blood test is yours, and shouldn't be arbitrarily dictated by your veterinarian.

There is a rule you can follow: If a vaccine is given at or before weaning time, boosters should be given at regular intervals and only the highest-quality vaccines should be used. Consult your veterinarian for further advice. The following preventable diseases are for your reference.

Canine Distemper (CD)

Distemper is rare today because of modern vaccine quality. This viral disease is always a danger; it is spread by contact or airborne respiratory droplets (coughs and sneezes) and is usually fatal to unvaccinated dogs. The reservoir of infection is located among city strays and rural coyotes and other canines. Signs of CD include coughing, lack of appetite, elevated body temperature, purulent nasal discharge, discolored teeth (in cases of distemper recovery), nervous twitching or convulsions, and death.

Canine Hepatitis, ICH, or CAV-1

This viral disease also can cause sudden death, sometimes without visible symptoms. ICH is basically a liver disease but other internal organs are affected as well. Exposure and signs are similar to those seen with CD plus jaundice and corneal edema, also known as blue eye.

Leptospirosis (Lepto)

Lepto is a kidney disease that is often spread by aquatic rodents. It's transmitted by infected urine, and signs include a roached or humped back caused by kidney pain, bloody or orange-colored urine, loss of appetite, and fever.

Kennel Cough or Tracheobronchitis

Kennel cough is caused by a number of bacteria including *Bordetella bronchiseptica,* and viruses that include parainfluenza, distemper, CAV-2, and possibly others. The affected dog coughs, hacks, and honks for several weeks before recovery. Antibiotics often are administered to prevent secondary opportunist infections, and sometimes cough suppressants are prescribed. Kennel cough should be monitored closely, because it stresses the entire respiratory system and can predispose the animal to pneumonia.

Parvovirus

Parvo is a potent, easily transmitted virus that's often fatal to susceptible puppies. In less acute infections, the signs are watery, often bloody diarrhea, vomiting, dehydration, high temperature, and sometimes cardiac complications. Signs often are absent in young puppies that suffer sudden heart failure without warning. Parvo often is spread by infected dogs' stools, even those that are several months old. Humans may act as vectors by stepping in infected stools and carrying the virus home. This virus is resistant to common disinfectants, and is one of the major reasons for not taking Duff out of his yard until he's immunized. Parvo's death rate is high without aggressive therapy, and even then it's significant, because there is no effective antiviral agent.

Coronavirus

To lay persons, coronavirus looks quite similar to parvo. The diseases can be differentiated by blood testing, but usually they're treated similarly. Prognosis is guarded in every case and the mortality rate is about the same as parvo.

Lyme Disease

Borrelia burgdorferi is the bacterium that causes Lyme disease. It was first diagnosed in Lyme, Connecticut, but has now spread to nearly every state. Lyme disease is transmitted by ticks and other bloodsucking parasites of deer, cattle, horses, elk, moose, dogs, cats, and humans. Typical signs include fever, sluggishness, joint pain with associated lameness, lymph node swelling, and loss of appetite. A specific blood test is available that will aid your veterinarian in diagnosing Lyme, and a vaccine is available.

Treatment is possible using a wide range of antibiotics, but early diagnosis is critical to success. Don't forget to minimize exposure by maximizing your tick prevention program. Lyme disease is a zoonotic disease (transmissible to humans).

Rabies

In 1997 the American Veterinary Medical Association (AVMA) reported 126 confirmed cases of rabies in dogs. Rabies reservoirs are found in warm-blooded animals, especially coyotes, foxes, raccoons, bats, ferrets, skunks, and wolves. This fatal disease remains continually present in most of North America, including the 48 contiguous states, Mexico, and Canada. The Centers for Disease Control (CDC) reported 6,280 cases of animal rabies during the first 10 months of 1999.

The rabies virus travels in nerve trunks from the bite site to the salivary glands, then to the brain, and the animal soon dies. One sign of infection is paralysis of the throat, resulting in copious stringy saliva drooling from the mouth. In *dumb* rabies, the dog staggers about until death. In *furious* rabies, the infected dog bites at the slightest provocation, whether the targets are animate or inanimate.

This is a zoonotic disease for which excellent vaccines are available. Pet vaccination is mandated by many local and federal ordinances, and wildlife are sometimes immunized by oral vaccines.

Parasites

Parasites are organisms that live on or within Duff's body, potentially causing harm to his health.

External Parasites

External parasites include fungi, mites, lice, fleas, and ticks that live on or in Duff's skin. Often called ringworm, fungi aren't associated with worms. Some fungi are transmissible to humans making their control even more signif-

icant. Topical fungus infection typically causes itchy, hairless, inflamed circular patterns or patchy lesions. It is diagnosed by culturing skin scrapings or by ruling out all other causes of skin lesions, and is treated with oral or topical fungicides.

Mange: Mange is caused by mite invasion into the animal's skin, usually causing alopecia (hair loss), erythema (redness), and irritation. Pruritus (itching) is usually associated with all

Cooling off on a hot day.

mange lesions either because of the invading mite's irritation or the secondary bacterial infection. *Demodex* (red mange) may be localized and cause less pruritus than the generalized and widespread infection. *Cheyletiella* (puppy dandruff), *Psoroptes* and *Sarcoptes* mite infestations are diagnosed by skin scrapings, and treated with dips, medicated baths, topical, or systemic miticides.

Ear mites: *Otodectes* (ear mites) are larger than their skin-oriented cousins and are suspected when dark wax exudes from Duff's ear canals. Infestation is confirmed by microscopic examination of the wax and is treated with systemic or topical miticides.

Lice: Louse infestation (pediculosis) is visible to the unaided eye. Louse eggs stick to

Westies have a healthy curiosity.

Healthy mothers produce healthy puppies.

the dog's back hair especially near his rump. When certain of the diagnosis, cure is effected by use of powders or shampoos containing safe insecticides.

Fleas: Fleas are the most common ectoparasite to cause inflammatory pruritus of canine skin. Found virtually everywhere dogs exist, heavier infestations thrive in warm, humid climates. Fleas are easy to treat but difficult to eradicate. They're secondary hosts for tapeworms, and their saliva may cause allergy. Fleas are easily found by passing a flea comb through Duff's rump hair or seeing their black comma-shaped feces on his skin. Fleas hop onto hosts, feed, mate, and lay eggs that are dropped on your carpet or lawn, and hatch into larvae that pupate into adults.

Flea control includes flea collars that generally are not effective. Use of premises flea bombs, topically applied sprays, powders, shampoos, or systemic medications are partially effective and have been used for decades. Newer systemic products may be given orally or applied to Duff's skin once a month. Seek veterinary advice about the type of product to use, its safety, cost, and effectiveness.

Biological flea control also is available, and may involve yard application of nontoxic nematodes (worms) that eat flea eggs or an insect growth regulator that interferes with the flea's life cycle. Don't use different products at the same time, during pregnancy, or without approval of Duff's veterinarian.

Ticks: Parasitic ticks bury their heads in their host's skin and suck blood for several days. Engorged female ticks often reach cherry size after a blood meal, but males are much smaller. After sucking blood the female detaches, lays thousands of eggs, and dies. Some ticks complete their entire life cycle on a dog (brown dog tick), or they may use other mammals as secondary hosts. Ticks are frequently found under the dog's collar or in his armpits.

Protect your own health with latex gloves because some tick-borne diseases can be transmitted to humans. Use tweezers to grasp the tick as close to Duff's skin as possible and detach it by gently pulling. Drop it into a container of alcohol, being careful not to squash or handle it with bare fingers (see Lyme Disease on page 67) If the tick's head breaks off, don't worry; it may cause a minor irritation but rarely a serious infection.

Internal Parasites

Ascarid: Ascarid (roundworm) larvae may remain hidden in cysts in Duff's tissues throughout his life. During pregnancy the encysted larvae migrate into unborn puppies that are thus born with roundworm infestation. Adult roundworms lay eggs that pass in the dog's feces and become sources of infestation for other dogs.

Hookworms: *Ancylostoma* (hookworm) thrives in warm climates. Eggs pass in the stool, hatch into larvae in the soil, which can penetrate the dog's skin. After entry, they migrate to the small intestine, molt to adults, which attach to the lining of the gut and suck blood. Hookworm signs include gut irritation, hemorrhage, and anemia. Puppies may die from heavy infestations.

Whipworms: *Trichuris* (whipworm) infestation is relatively uncommon and produces obscure signs. Adults live in an outpouching of the large intestine and predisposes the animal to unthriftiness or chronic diarrhea. Aggressive treatment and regular laboratory examinations are advised to be sure this parasite is eradicated.

Coccidia: Coccidia are microscopic protozoan parasites that live in dogs' intestines. Infestation can cause chronic, bloody diarrhea, but treatment with a systemic medicine usually is successful.

Diagnosis of all of the above parasites is possible by fecal examination and a veterinarian should prescribe treatment.

Tapeworms: Tapeworms require two hosts and can't be transmitted directly from dog to dog. Fleas, mammals, or birds may serve as secondary hosts and to become infested, Duff must eat part of the carcass of a secondary host. Tapeworm heads attach to the lining of the host's intestine, and the worm's segmented body grows to a great length. Treating tapeworms is only half the battle because controlling the dog's consumption of secondary host material is equally important.

Diagnosis is made by finding tiny white segments attached to Duff's anal hair or on the surface of his stool, and oral medication is used for treatment.

Heartworm: Heartworm larvae *(Dirofilaria)* are picked up by a mosquito when the insect sucks blood from an infested dog. When the mosquito penetrates a susceptible dog, some larvae are transmitted. An adult heartworm may reach a foot (30 cm) in length where it lives in the dog's heart and major arteries. Circulatory failure may occur in a heavy infestation and an infected dog is a reservoir of infestation for other dogs.

Before a preventive program is begun a blood test must show that no larvae are circulating in Duff's bloodstream. Heartworm prevention is accomplished by means of monthly oral medication.

Parasite Prevention and Treatment

Treating every puppy for worms, whether or not infestation exists, is a perilous procedure. Worm killers are poisons and a responsible Westie owner should rely on a veterinarian to diagnose and prescribe worm therapy. Ask your veterinarian about the practicality, safety, and efficacy of oral drugs that will prevent heartworm and most of the internal parasites discussed above.

Nonpreventable Diseases

Some important conditions require early diagnosis and therapy but can't be prevented by vaccine or careful husbandry.

Diabetes Mellitus

So-called sugar diabetes is a metabolic disease caused by an insulin deficiency. Insulin is a hormone secreted by the pancreas that allows glucose utilization. Diabetes occurs in all breeds and is often seen in obese, middle-aged females. Its early signs are lethargy, excessive water consumption, increased urination, and weight gain. Untreated, the course of the disease is marked by sudden weight loss, vomiting, and coma. If you suspect diabetes in Duff, see his veterinarian. This disease is treatable, but success depends on early diagnosis.

Atopy

Allergic skin disease called atopy is seen in many breeds. It's manifested as a nonparasitic itch affecting young adults. It may be seasonally associated with pollen inhalation, ingestion, or contact, any of which causes severe pruritus (itch) and skin inflammation.

Often, atopy isn't diagnosed because of failure to recognize that an ingested or inhaled allergen can cause dramatic itching symptoms. Pruritus also can be associated with an irritant that touches the skin of the feet, flanks, or armpits, and sometimes is mistreated by using soothing, drying, or moisturizing skin remedies before professional help is sought.

Hereditary Conditions

Double Dentition

Double teeth may be the result of downsizing some breeds, which includes smaller jaws, but genetic predisposition to double teeth is theorized in most small breeds and is relatively common in Westies. A double set of teeth results when a puppy's deciduous (temporary) teeth aren't shed promptly when permanent teeth emerge through the gums. A single tooth or many may be involved shortly after three months of age. Double incisors rarely cause difficulty but double canine teeth (fangs), which erupt at about six months of age, may present more serious problems.

As Duff's permanent teeth erupt you'll notice bits of food and strands of hair caught between the baby and the permanent teeth. Brushing his teeth will help but isn't the answer to this problem.

Check the number of retained teeth and their solidity, and call your veterinarian. If the permanent teeth are solid and well aligned, and retained teeth are loose, you may be advised to daily wiggle them with your finger until they're shed. If the permanent teeth are growing awry, extraction of deciduous teeth may be necessary. Ignoring the early double dentition may result in deformity of Duff's bite or gingivitis and loss of his permanent teeth.

Legg-Calvé-Perthes Disease

When a portion of the femoral head degenerates (dies) before normal bone maturity, the technical term applied is femoral head *aseptic necrosis*. Occurrence of this hereditary disease in Westies is significant. It usually appears between six and eight months of age and is most easily recognized when Duff is moving across the floor.

Often, it causes chronic, intermittent lameness that may be overlooked because of its insidious onset. This disease causes *grade two* lameness (relatively minor), when a fracture or thorn in the foot represents *grade four* (more dynamic lameness). Hind lameness that's unrelated to injury is suspicious and veterinary examination reveals pain upon manipulation of the hip joint and shrinking of the upper thigh muscles. Temperament changes may be noted before pain is manifested. Although a puppy's personality

A big backyard is great, but play is a participation sport.

*Your puppy's parents should have been
screened for hereditary diseases.*

rarely is permanently affected, Duff may
become quieter and resent being picked up or
cuddled. X-ray imaging is diagnostic.

Mild cases often respond to several months
of forced rest. Surgical removal of the femoral
head and formation of a false joint sometimes
helps severe cases. Once affected, Duff may
show slight or pronounced lameness for life. If
ignored altogether, arthritic changes in the
degenerating joint may be quite painful, or
they may be self-limiting.

Craniomandibular Osteopathy (CMO)

CMO or Lion Jaw has been recognized in
canine literature for many years. It's a non-
cancerous, proliferative bone growth along
both mandibles (lower jawbones), other skull
bones, and occasionally forearm bones. Manifested by bony enlargement of the mandible
during its formative stage, CMO occurs in
Westies, Scotties, and Cairns, and is a serious
but treatable genetic disease. Its usual onset
occurs between three months and one year
of age.

CMO causes drooling, difficulty opening the
mouth, pain when eating, and often a slight
fever. The disease often is suspected when
Duff's jaw is palpated at the time of vaccination and X-ray confirms the diagnosis. CMO
may be self-limiting and progress stops at the
time of physical maturity. The bony change
interferes with eating and may cause death if
it progresses without intervention.

Antiinflammatory drugs usually are successful in treating this disease but it must be

regularly monitored and therapy continued until bone growth is complete. When treated, the bony swelling often recedes but some enlargement and impaired chewing may continue for the rest of the dog's life.

Globoid Cell Leukodystrophy (GCL)

GCL is a paralytic nervous system disease affecting the protective myelin sheath that surrounds the spinal cord nerves. Leukodystrophy is rare and also is reported in the Cairn Terrier. It's believed to be genetically transmitted and is usually seen shortly after weaning or by six months of age. Principal GCL signs are hind leg partial paralysis accompanied by loss of coordination, and sometimes by tremors of the body, head, and tail. No treatment is presently recognized and this paralytic disease is believed to always follow a rather definite, progressive course ending in death.

Copper Toxicosis

Some Westies are born with genetically faulty copper metabolism, allowing this mineral to build up and cause degeneration of the liver. Liver cirrhosis often progresses gradually and the condition is well advanced before outward signs are seen. It is usually diagnosed in adults under four years of age when hepatitis symptoms appear. Typical signs are mucous membrane and skin jaundice accompanied by loss of appetite and abdominal pain. Further evidence of liver disease is indicated by laboratory tests, and a liver biopsy will specifically diagnose the disease.

Specific drugs are administered to reduce the amount of copper retained within the liver and will rehabilitate Duff to a near-normal life, but death will occur if he isn't quickly diagnosed and treated.

Luxated Patella (Kneecap Dislocation)

Hereditary predisposition marks this deformity that's prevalent in small breeds and only occasionally seen in Westies. Anatomically, lower ends of the femur (thighbone), and the upper end of the tibia or shinbone are malformed and the groove in which the patella slides is quite shallow. Also, the ligaments holding the patella in place often are weak and the angulation between the femur and tibia is poor. The result is an unstable stifle (knee joint) that may dislocate when Duff plays or jumps. It usually occurs in a young adult, sometimes before maturity, but occasionally in a four- or five-year-old.

A minor twisting action causes the patella to luxate, resulting in pain and lameness. Sometimes an affected dog hops on three legs for a while, then gradual use returns. The patella may return to its normal position and lameness is intermittent thereafter.

Several surgical treatments are proven successful and the specific operation prescribed depends on the joint's condition and the specific bones and ligaments involved.

Epilepsy

Sometimes an inherited convulsive disorder, epilepsy may also be caused by brain injury or tumors, or central nervous system infections. Hereditary seizures usually begin when Duff is several years old, making epilepsy difficult to eradicate from a bloodline when young dogs are bred.

Early signs are obscure and brief. Duff may stand as if bewildered for several minutes, then return to normal. Later, he may stagger, faint, lie still, and rise to wobbly legs before quickly recovering. Still later, he may fall and lie on his side with neck arched, paddling all four feet for several minutes or hours. Veterinarians often diagnose the condition by described signs but in some cases the seizure lasts longer and a seizuring dog is seen by a veterinarian.

Epileptic seizures usually are treated successfully with oral medication, but no cure is known. If untreated, the seizures may become more frequent and more severe and eventually cause death by suffocation and respiratory paralysis.

Miscellaneous Genetically Related Diseases

Pyruvate Kinase Deficiency (PK)

This rare Westie blood disorder results in loss of energy, pale mucous membranes, weakness, and lethargy. Onset is between four months and one year of age, but is difficult to evaluate until later, when the physical weakness becomes increasingly evident. X-rays showing increased bone density are somewhat diagnostic and may differentiate this disease from other blood deficiency disorders. PK is believed to be genetic in origin and occasionally is successfully treated by bone marrow transplants.

Epidermal Dysplasia

A rare genetic Westie condition is a generalized dermatological disease sometimes called armadillo skin. Epidermal dysplasia causes skin thickening, redness, and intense itching, primarily of the feet, legs, and abdomen. Disease progress includes lost hair, hardened skin, and dark pigmentation, and the skin takes on the appearance of a Texas armadillo's back. Treatment is usually futile, but minor success may be achieved with steroid use.

Juvenile Cataracts

This inherited problem and certain other ocular diseases occasionally occur in Westies. Cataracts of young adults can be surgically treated by veterinary ophthalmologists.

Keratitis Sicca (KS)

Often called dry-eye syndrome, this disease may be incurable but can be treated and an affected dog maintained for many years by use of eyedrops and ophthalmic ointments. Certain surgical procedures may improve the condition as well. KS may predispose the animal to conjunctivitis and corneal ulcers.

Congenital Deafness

Congenital deafness occurs occasionally in Westies, and cure is unlikely. We must hasten to add that deafness isn't a fair reason for giving Duff up; if you have patience and are a clever trainer, deaf Westies make excellent pets.

WESTIE VOCATIONS AND AVOCATIONS

Your relationship with Tammy as a companion and housemate is directly related to her contentment in your home and is dependent upon shared activities. It's possible that playing with her in your yard, taking her for walks in the park, and other unstructured, enjoyable hobbies are sufficient, but sometimes you both need more variety.

A few canine avocations are listed here and described briefly for your consideration. All these activities require close cooperation and communication between dog and owner. In every event the key to mastering the activity is Tammy's desire and ability to focus on you and please you. If you want to teach her, try one or more of these activities. Start by attending competitive events, buy a book, join a club, and give it a try.

Agility

Agility is a competitive sport in which dogs run an obstacle course, and the one that completes it within the designated time with the fewest errors wins. Agility trials are splendid spectator sports, drawing huge audiences of interested onlookers. Many all-breed clubs sponsor agility trials, and hundreds of agility

Obedience classes teach you to train your Westie.

clubs have formed to promote the sport. Agility training is fun and entertaining, even if you don't compete in formal trials for ribbons, trophies, and titles.

Many owners have found agility training to be a means of correcting attention deficits in bored dogs. A team consists of a person and a dog. You're free to run the course at your own pace, and unless you're practicing for a timed trial, you needn't hurry. The dog must have a biddable temperament and some obedience training is essential before she's worked off lead in the same arena as other dogs. Training for her sport can start in your backyard or inside the house when Tammy is a puppy, because in the beginning it's all a game and accuracy is more important than speed.

Props and Obstacles

Agility props and obstacles are sized according to the height of the dog. Jumps, an A-frame to climb over, and an elevated dog walk are set up. A teetering seesaw to walk across, a table to pause on, and fabric tunnels are also included. A line of poles to weave, a suspended window frame and hanging tire to jump through are all included in agility obstacles.

Use a snug, web buckle collar, and a short, lightweight nylon leash and some tasty morsel inducements. Keep a small treat in your signal-hand to maintain Tammy's concentration on that hand. Practice before meals because delicious enticements are more meaningful when she's hungry.

Tunnel: Start training with a tunnel that's easily constructed from an old sheet and a couple of chairs. Start Tammy in one end, tell her *"Through,"* and simultaneously wave her through with a hand signal. Or, crawl through the tunnel, enticing Tammy to follow. When she's made it through, tell her *"Good dog,"* give her a treat, take a break, and try it again.

Elevated dog walk: Another simple obstacle is the elevated dog walk. A plank is cut to the specified size, the ends are painted, and it's placed flat on the ground. Encourage Tammy to walk the entire length, getting on and off the plank only on the colored ends. After she learns to walk the plank without hesitation, raise it the thickness of a brick, then to the height of a cinderblock. Don't let her make a mistake. Keep her on the plank by constantly steadying her with the leash, speaking to her and supporting her. Maintain her concentration on walking the plank with a morsel of food held in your hand before her eyes. Hurdles and jumps of all types should be reserved for a later date when Tammy is fully developed. Training can begin when Tammy is still an energetic pup; however, don't progress too rapidly or she'll tire and lose interest in the game.

Communicating

You can communicate with her continually, but in a trial you can't touch her at any time. Give short verbal directions and Tammy will identify the words used with the desired actions and the hand signals. Plainly point your open hand and fingers at the obstacle, and command Tammy to *"Take it," "Jump," "Over,"* or *"Through."* Be consistent and positive and don't give multiword or unclear commands. A command must be obeyed before the expected treat is awarded. Have patience, don't nag or scold, and always praise her when she succeeds.

This activity is a superb means of playing with your Westie. Eventually, you may be interested in formal agility trials and titles. For further information, contact the AKC or the United States Dog Agility Association (see Information, page 92).

Conformation Showing

If you purchased a show-quality dog and she matures into a vision of perfection, you'll undoubtedly wish to enter her in a conformation show. Before you take that step, ask an experienced breeder-handler or judge to fault her, or compare her conformation with the standard. If advised to wait a few months or longer before beginning, take heart; maturity may complete an already beautiful specimen. If you're encouraged, obtain a copy of AKC show rules and attend several all-breed shows.

Remember that Tammy is a terrier; outward appearance is only part of her genetic quality. If she doesn't have a Highlander's temperament, carriage, and movement, she shouldn't contribute to the West Highland White gene pool.

Conformation shows' goals are to recognize Westies that most nearly match the breed's standard of perfection.

Sometimes handlers make more mistakes than their dogs. The logical approach to dog showing is to learn from experts all you can about Westie conformation, grooming, and handling. Attend many shows and learn what's required of show dogs, but especially watch experienced handlers and winning Westies. Teach Tammy basic good manners while she's a puppy and join a showmanship class sponsored by your Westie club. A qualified instructor will teach you to properly exhibit Tammy before a judge. In the company of other owners and their Westies you'll learn the best technique to handle Tammy's lead, attain a perfect gait, and the best stance. By experience, you'll learn to maintain her interest and exhibit her to show her strongest points.

Fun matches are informal conformation shows in which no championship points are awarded. They're instructional tools for new dogs and beginning handlers. In a fun match, an owner exhibits the Westie in the same manner as required in a point show, but pressure is reduced. Showing Tammy in matches will teach her to tolerate and ignore other dogs and people in the ring and gallery. Ask each match judge why you won or lost.

Points

Under AKC show rules, points are awarded to the winners in certain categories. A major win is one in which three to five points are awarded. Once Tammy has won two majors and at least fifteen points, in at least three different shows, under at least three different judges, she's awarded the Champion of Record

title. If she has qualities of perfection, and you are an excellent handler, sooner or later, she will no longer be just Tammy, she'll be "Ch. Tammy McTavish," and that day you'll walk on air.

Canine Good Citizens (CGC)

Anyone interested in canine welfare should look into the CGC program. Here is a set of simple tasks that owners can teach their Westies, that enhance the bond between owner and dog. The CGC title is recognized by the AKC, and can be won by every Westie that learns good manners. There is no competition between dogs. An officer of an AKC-approved dog club will administer and evaluate Tammy's performance, and if she passes, she will be awarded a certificate. Tammy should know some simple, practical obedience commands before starting this project.

Agility trials test trainability.

The Good Citizen test involves ten different tasks, each of which you can teach Tammy without professional help, or if you prefer, many all-breed dog clubs conduct classes. Practical exercises are included such as walking through a crowd, meeting other owners accompanied by their dogs, and walking in places where shopping carts, wheelchairs, or crutches are found. CGC is a very worthwhile project for both you and Tammy, and if you're interested, you can learn more about this plan by contacting the AKC.

Obedience

Another team sport you and Tammy might enjoy is obedience work. Trials are judged on a dog's ability to follow her owner's commands,

A good Westie is always a winner.

Westies love to show off in public.

Getting the message at a terrier trial.

Contemporary terrier trials are humane exhibits.

A natural-born ham and proud of it.

Canine Good Citizen tests stress canine socialization.

and are part of most all-breed shows. Obedience training serves several important functions. It strengthens the bond between you and your Westie and in so doing, increases your enjoyment of your companion. Obedience provides for the safety and happiness of your dog by teaching rules of conduct. It intensifies the instinctive pack order that's natural for all dogs and places you in a leadership role, which is necessary for amity and harmony in a human family. Obedience disciplines tend to produce good companion dogs that create a pleasant relationship in your neighborhood. If obedience training can accomplish all that, it's certainly well worth your time!

Obedience competition is a formal continuation of the good manners training discussed previously. Some obedience exercises go far beyond simple *come, sit,* and *stay,* to include these exercises plus heeling on and off lead, retrieval of objects and tracking. Successful obedience trial participation is enormously gratifying to both you and Tammy and each title earned seems to stimulate the team to strive for the next.

Formal obedience work begins after Tammy is six months old with a Sub-Novice or Novice level and progresses through Novice Open, and Utility levels leading to the titles Companion Dog (CD), Companion Dog Excellent (CDX), Utility Dog (UD), Utility Dog Excellent (UDX), Tracking Dog (TD), and finally the Obedience Trial Champion (OTCH).

Successful obedience competition is proof that you and Tammy are partners. She can't earn a title without your training and participation. Westies aren't famous for obedience work, but they can hold their own with proper schooling. For more information, contact your Westie club, all-breed club, the AKC, or search the Internet.

Terrier Trials

Westies are hunters, bred to go to ground after badger, fox, and other vermin. The AKC has devised earthdog tests to provide simulated burrowing for game. By her response, Tammy's tenacity and working ability is judged. The course consists of man-made underground passages, complete with bends, scents, and dens. Three AKC titles may be won in progressive fashion from the Junior Earthdog (JE) to the intermediate level Senior Earthdog (SE) title, then to the Master Earthdog (ME) title. To earn each of these titles Tammy must exhibit and earn points in two to four separate tests under three different judges.

The American Working Terrier Association (AWTA) also sponsors terrier trials that are open to all terriers and are also designed to test hunting skills in simulated field conditions. Those that perform to required standards receive an AWTA Certificate of Gameness as proof of their instinctive ability and their training.

The principal difference between earthdog tests and other avocations discussed is that success in this task is little influenced by the skill of the trainer, because earthdog tests judge the instincts of your Westie more than her trainability. Some claim that an earthdog title is the ultimate accomplishment for a Westie, because it is the basis for her development. Regardless of your opinion on this subject, the indisputable fact is that earthdog competition gives Tammy something to do. It helps satisfy her need for supervised exercise, and may be a source of gratification for you.

Therapy Dogs

Therapy dogs aren't dogs that just happen into a nursing home, hospital, hospice, or care center. They're well-mannered dogs that like people. In the role of therapy dog, Tammy may sit quietly beside an elderly lady, loving the petting she's dispensing, or she may fetch a ball for a special child. Tammy is trained to make the day a little brighter for shut-ins, to lift their spirits, and motivate incapacitated people to interact.

A small therapy dog can charm an Alzheimer's patient in a day care center or light up the eyes of an elderly and incapacitated gent in a nursing home. The friendly Westie is custom-made to bridge the gap between reality and the incognizant minds of these unfortunate people.

Some residents miss their own dogs enormously, and in a Westie's soft eyes they recall their favorite dog and relive past good times. In Tammy's affectionate tongue these people remember the devoted response they received from their dogs.

Tammy delivers and receives pleasure each time you take him to an institution. She brings joy to some hapless person and in turn, relishes the attention she receives, and you will experience the satisfaction of sharing your Westie.

The Delta Society is one of the groups that serve as an international resource for the human-animal bond. It is dedicated to expand the awareness of the positive effect animals can have on human health. The society's goal is to research and provide the beneficial effect pets bring to the general population and particularly, how these pets positively affect human health and well-being. It publishes a number of newsletters and a home study course for volunteers who are interested in therapy visitation programs.

In addition to having an even temperament, therapy dogs must be more than one year old, healthy, well groomed, up-to-date on immunizations, and responsive to fundamental obedience commands. Tammy should be certified by an agency such as the Delta Society or Therapy Dogs International, both of which also provide liability insurance and temperament testing.

Therapy dogs are invaluable to care center patients.

Fun-loving Duff is fortunate in having a long lifeline. With good nutrition, loving care, and lacking any accident or devastating illness, he can expect to enjoy your company for 12 or 14 years.

Health Problems in Old Westies

Arthritis

Osteoarthritis is Duff's worst enemy; his hips are most likely to be affected, but virtually every joint may be a source of pain. Prescription products may be used or over-the-counter drugs such as ibuprofen and buffered aspirin may relieve the inflammatory pain. Acetaminophen also may be used when other products cause digestive upsets but no drug should be used without your veterinarian's approval. Liver-flavored glucosamine and chondroitin capsules in combination with the antioxidant vitamin C often help, and geriatric multivitamins may be beneficial as well.

Lumps and Bumps

Old Westies' faces and legs sometimes develop benign wartlike tumors or skin cysts. Occasionally, fatty tumors lurk just under his abdominal or chest skin. Treatment

Senior Westies need more loving care and understanding.

depends on the size and position of these lumps as well as on Duff's age and general health. Your veterinarian may elect to monitor them if Duff is quite old and the lumps aren't causing pain.

Blindness and Cataracts

Nuclear sclerosis is the clouding of an old dog's lenses, which appear similar to cataracts. Rarely does this lens clouding cause total blindness, although low-light vision usually is impaired. Successful lens extraction can be performed by veterinary ophthalmologists but the operation is different and the risk is greater than in the human operation.

Deafness

Hearing gradually diminishes with age, but some of Duff's deafness may be more of a convenience and falls under the category of selective hearing. He pretends he doesn't hear you call when responding will be a chore for him or when he's busy napping.

Obesity

Obesity and its accompanying stresses may be caused by overfeeding or it could be a sign of several serious metabolic diseases such as diabetes, hypothyroidism, or Cushing's disease. Schedule a veterinary examination to rule out systemic diseases. If Duff is simply overweight, begin a careful reducing plan using a special low-calorie dog food that contains complete, balanced nutrition. Sometimes months or years may be added to his life by weight reduction.

Memory Loss

Canine Cognitive Dysfunction is a recognized old dog problem in which Duff may forget his training. He may urinate or defecate in strange new places or forget where his bed is located. Make an appointment for a physical exam to rule out other diseases. Sometimes a new memory drug will be of value, but often memory loss will respond to regular trips to the toilet area, frequent short walks, and praise when he urinates in appropriate places.

Incontinence

Urinary incontinence is a common old Westie problem. Lack of urinary control may be associated with a metabolic disease or cognitive dysfunction, but often it's simply the result of tired old muscles. When nerves controlling bladder muscles degenerate, Duff can't control voiding and will leak urine when asleep and sometimes even when he's walking across the room. Females seem to be affected more frequently than males.

Frequent trips to his toilet area will certainly help resolve this problem, but scolding or attempted retraining is rarely effective. Plastic-backed sleeping mats make incontinence manageable and prolong his enjoyment of life because some incontinent dogs seem to be embarrassed by their condition.

Euthanasia

Just like housebreaking and leash training, it's your responsibility to provide Duff with the final act of kindness. If life has become too painful to endure and enjoyment is nonexistent, discuss euthanasia with your veterinarian but don't hurry the decision. The reason for giving your old friend a painless departure from the world is associated with a single factor: Life has become an overwhelmingly painful, confusing burden.

In my many years of veterinary practice I euthanized many dogs and never became steeled to the procedure, but I learned that euthanasia isn't cruel when it's approached tenderly and with understanding and compassion for the owner as well as the pet. It's the final act of love and kindness you can provide for Duff. He will suffer no pain or anxiety when the lethal injection is given. Call his veterinarian to find out if it's possible to take him

Never leave an older Westie alone at its final moments.

CHECKLIST

Senior Westie

Sharing your life with a dog that will probably live to a ripe old age is a wonderful prospect. However, one day your Westie friend will no longer be young, his needs will change, and he will need you now more than ever. That's what friends are for.

1 If your aging Westie seems to have greater difficulty moving as freely as he once did, arthritis might be the cause. There are a number of possible therapies, but before administering any pain-reliever, consult your veterinarian about which to use and the correct dosage to administer.

2 The appearance of skin growths is a common sign of aging. While many growths will be more unsightly than dangerous, they should be monitored carefully and any change brought to your veterinarian's attention. With some dogs, surgery might bring on unnecessary stress.

3 Like aging people, aging dogs often experience diminished eyesight, though total blindness is not common. Surgical treatment is available, but involves risk. Thousands of dogs that lose some or all of their eyesight function surprisingly well as long as they remain in familiar surroundings.

4 Many old dogs will experience hearing loss, but before seeking treatment you should determine whether a delayed response to your call is from impending deafness or due to the type of deep sleep seen among aging dogs.

5 Overweight in an older pet may be the symptom of a disease or result from a lack of exercise. If you and your veterinarian have ruled out systemic diseases, your Westie must go on a reducing diet. Weight loss may add precious time to your relationship with your pet.

6 Older dogs may forget their training or certain habit patterns. If your dog shows such behavior, have your veterinarian check him to rule out any disease process. You will probably have to do some retaining or make more trips to his toilet area.

7 If your dog develops incontinence, you will have to adjust the household routine to allow for it. Training will not help here, as your dog cannot control the problem. Many incontinent seniors are embarrassed by the condition, but it helps if your dog knows you still love him. He needs your patient tolerance.

to the clinic before office hours so there will be no wait. Stay with him if you can handle the grief. He'll appreciate having you nearby and your presence will assure him that you haven't abandoned him.

The injection should be prepared in advance and his veterinarian will handle him gently and calmly, speaking to him in comforting tones. Either you or an assistant will steady him as the clinician makes a quick venipuncture and

Older Westies still like to rule their turf.

Don't force exercise on a senior citizen.

like a lantern that's used all its fuel, Duff's life flickers and is painlessly gone in an instant.

Life Goes On

Bury your pet's body at home, in a pet cemetery, or arrange for cremation if that's more practical but don't bury yourself in his grave. Don't waste your life with perpetual grieving and despair; instead, remember that Duff's life was filled with happiness and he brought you years of joy.

Don't search for Duff's clone when you're ready for a new dog; there isn't another Westie in the world exactly like him! You will soon find this out with a newcomer. Don't put undue pressure on your new companion and don't expect him to fill Duff's role.

Senior Westies appreciate their creature comforts.

Besides a good understanding of Duff's physical aging problems, his mental status needs to be comprehended. Canine senility isn't much different from the human counterpart. Duff may momentarily forget where his food or water pans are. Don't hesitate to lead him to it when he acts confused or doesn't respond immediately to feeding time. He may lie in strange places, forgetting what his bed is for and lying beside it on the hard floor. He may refuse his normal food, probably because of a loss of normal scenting. He may become snappy toward his well-known family, possibly because of fear of being roughly handled or picked up. Generally it's best to limit access to your aging Westie when small children visit.

Measures to Take to Enhance Your Old Westie's Life

When he has reached the age of ten, initiate these measures to enhance his golden years, and lengthen his vitality.

✔ Take him to your veterinarian at least every six months for a geriatric examination and laboratory work-up when necessary.

✔ Examine and clean his eyes of any accumulation of mucus. Contact your veterinarian if any pus is seen and ask about clipping the hair around his eyes.

✔ Discuss senile cataracts and ask about the need for surgery, costs, and success rate.

✔ Ask your veterinarian about medication to relieve arthritis pain. Be sure you understand the dosage prescribed and all potential side effects.

✔ Keep the hair on his chin trimmed shorter than usual to avoid dampness and infection caused by increased drooling.

✔ Heat his food slightly to increase its aroma and stimulate his appetite.

✔ Ask your pet food dealer to suggest a geriatric diet to compensate for his decreased digestive function.

✔ Ask your veterinarian about geriatric vitamin supplements to improve his general health and appetite.

✔ Regularly examine his mouth for gum tumors, tartar build-up, bad breath, and loose teeth.

✔ Accompany him to the toilet area of the yard and stay with him while he urinates and defecates. Watch for any abnormal color in the urine and frequency of urination. Also, be alert for abnormal

Furnish a coat for cool weather walking.

FOR YOUR OLD WESTIE

bowel movements such as diarrhea, constipation, or loss of control.

✔ Provide thick plastic-backed rugs or bathmats to sleep on, and wash them frequently.

✔ Pad his favorite napping places to help prevent decubital (pressure) ulcers or bedsores.

✔ Keep him on rough surfaces and trim his nails frequently to prevent slipping.

✔ Clap your hands or stomp your foot to announce your presence before touching him.

Help your senior Westie up and down stairs.

✔ Gently lift his hindquarters when he rises to alleviate stress on his old joints.

✔ Provide ramps (commercially available) to reduce the stress of climbing up steps.

✔ Take him for frequent short walks and never urge him to continue when he prefers to rest.

✔ When you take him for walks give him nudges together with your verbal directions.

✔ Buy or knit a sweater for his walks on cool, rainy, snowy, or cloudy days.

✔ Mix his food with no-fat beef or chicken broth to increase its palatability.

✔ Give him small quantities of food twice or three times daily, taking care not to overfeed.

✔ Be sure he always has plenty of fresh water in a clean bowl.

✔ Keep the hair on his bottom clipped short to prevent feces from collecting.

Westie Information Web Addresses
West Highland White Home Page
http://www.dsv.nv~sannie/whlinks_.html

West Highland White Terrier Club of America
http://www.westieclubamerica.com/

West Highland White Breed Standard
http://.akc.org/breeds/recbreeds/westie.cfm

West Highland White Terrier Breeders Directory
*http://www.cheta.net/connect/canine/
Director/westhigh.htm*

West Highland White Terrier Directory
*http://puppyshop.com/caninebreeds/Westie/
htm*

AKC Earthdog Tests
*http://members.tripod.com/~Jerrier/
Earthdog.html/*

American Working Terrier Association
http://www.dirt-dog.com/awta/

Organizations
American Kennel Club
5580 Centerview Drive, Suite 200
Raleigh, NC 27606-3390

United Kennel Club (UKC)
100 E. Kilgore Rd
Kalamazoo, MI 49001-5598

Books
Cleland, Sheila. *Pet Owner's Guide to the West Highland White Terrier.* Lydney, Glos., England: Ringpress Books Ltd, 1997.
Dunbar, Ian. *The Essential West Highland White Terrier.* New York: Macmillan General Reference, 1999.
Faherty, Ruth. *Westies, from Head to Tail.* Loveland, CO: Alpine Publications, 2001.
Gentry, Daphne. *The New West Highland White Terrier.* New York: Howell Book House, 1998.
Martin, Dawn. *A New Owner's Guide to West Highland White Terriers.* Neptune City, NJ: TFH Publications, 1996.
Killick, Robert. *West Highland White: An Owner's Guide.* New York: HarperCollins, 1999.
Weiss, Seymour. *The West Highland White Terrier: An Owner's Guide to a Happy, Healthy Westie.* New York: Macmillan Publishing Company, 1996.

References
American Kennel Club. *The Complete Dog Book.* New York: Howell Book House, 1997.
Clark, Ross D. and Joan R. Stainer. *Medical and Genetic Aspects of Purebred Dogs II.* St. Simons Island, GA: Forum Publications, Inc., 1994.
Lorenz, Michael D. and Larry M. Cornelius. *Small Animal Medical Diagnosis.* Philadelphia: J.B. Lippincott Company, 1993.

The Scottish Terrier (right) and the West Highland White Terrier have common roots, but are separate breeds.

Those good looks justify the grooming needed.

Westies know just how to handle their star quality.

About the Author

Dan Rice practiced veterinary medicine most of his life in Colorado. A few years ago he and his wife Marilyn retired to Arizona where he began a free-lance writing career. He has kept busy evaluating book proposals and manuscripts for Barron's and has written several as-yet unpublished works of fiction. *Westies* is his thirteenth book published by Barron's. His other titles include *Bengal Cats, Complete Book of Dog Breeding, Complete Book of Cat Breeding, Akitas, Dogs from A to Z (A Dictionary of Canine Terms), The Well-Mannered Cat, Brittanys, Chesapeake Bay Retrievers, Training Your German Shepherd, The Dog Handbook, The Beagle Handbook,* and *Big Dog Breeds.* Dan keeps abreast of pet research and the fancy through study and writing.

Photo Credits

Kent and Donna Dannen: pages 2, 8 top left, 8 top right, 8 bottom, 9 top, 12, 13, 16, 17, 21, 24, 28 bottom, 29, 32, 33, 36 top, 36 bottom left, 36 bottom right, 37, 40, 41, 44 bottom, 52 top left, 52 top right, 52 bottom, 53, 56, 60 top, 60 bottom right, 61 top, 64, 65, 68 top, 69, 73, 76, 77, 80 top, 80 bottom left, 80 bottom right, 81 top left, 81 top right, 81 bottom left, 81 bottom right, 84, 85, 88, 89 top, 89 bottom, 93 top left, 93 top right, 93 bottom left; Pets by Paulette: pages 4, 5, 20, 25, 45, 48, 49, 57, 93 bottom right; Tara Darling: pages 9 bottom left, 9 bottom right, 28 top, 44 top, 60 bottom left, 61 bottom, 68 bottom, 72.

Important Note

This book is concerned with selecting, keeping, and raising West Highland White Terriers. The publisher and the author think it is important to point out that the advice and information for West Highland White Terrier maintenance applies to healthy, normally developed animals. Anyone who acquires an adult dog or one from an animal shelter must consider that the animal may have behavioral problems and may, for example, bite without any visible provocation. Such anxiety biters are dangerous for the owner as well as the general public.

Caution is further advised in the association of children with dogs, in meetings with other dogs, and in exercising the dog without a leash.

Dedication and Acknowledgments

To the lovely lady who boosts me toward my destiny in the roles of Mentor and Nemesis, proof-reader and critic, friend and partner: my perfect wife Marilyn. I'm indebted to Seymour Weiss, a fellow dog lover, a successful Westie breeder, exhibitor, terrier judge, Westie author, and a professional editor at Barron's.

Cover Photos

Front cover: Norvia Behling; Back cover: Tara Darling; Inside front cover: Pets by Paulette; Inside back cover: Kent and Donna Dannen

© Copyright 2002 by Barron's Educational Series, Inc.

All inquiries should be addressed to:
Barron's Educational Series, Inc.
250 Wireless Boulevard
Hauppauge, NY 11788
http://www.barronseduc.com

Library of Congress Catalog Card No. 2001035267

ISBN-13: 978-0-7641-1899-9
ISBN-10: 0-7641-1899-4

Library of Congress Cataloging-in-Publication Data
Rice, Dan, 1933–
 West Highland white terriers : everything about purchase, care, nutrition, breeding, and health care / Dan Rice ; illustrations by Michelle Earle-Bridges.
  p. cm. — (A Complete pet owner's manual)
 Includes bibliographical references (p.).
 ISBN 0-7641-1899-4 (alk. paper)
 1. West Highland white terrier. I. Title. II. Series.
SF429.W4 R53 2002
636.755—dc21   2001035267

Printed in China
14 13 12 11 10